The River Lock

The River Lock

One Boy's Life along the Mohawk

Stephen Haven

SYRACUSE UNIVERSITY PRESS

Copyright © 2008 by Syracuse University Press
Syracuse, New York 13244-5160
All Rights Reserved
First Edition 2008
08 09 10 11 12 13   6 5 4 3 2 1

Title page: The St. Ann's Episcopal Church Men and Boys Choir, circa 1964. Courtesy of St. Ann's Episcopal Church, Amsterdam, New York.

Permission to reprint the following excerpts is gratefully acknowledged: "Bad Moon Rising" by John Fogerty. Copyright © 1969 Jondora Music (BMI). Copyright renewed. Courtesy of Concord Music Group, Inc. All rights reserved. Used by permission. "Proud Mary" by John Fogerty. Copyright © 1968 Jondora Music (BMI). Copyright renewed. Courtesy of Concord Music Group, Inc. All rights reserved. Used by permission. "Awakened" from *New and Collected Poems: 1931–2001* by Czeslaw Milosz. Copyright © 1988, 1991, 1995, 2001 by Czeslaw Milosz Royalties, Inc. Reprinted by permission of HarperCollins Publishers. Excerpt from "Little Gidding" in *Four Quartets*, copyright 1942 by T. S. Eliot and renewed 1970 by Esme Valerie Eliot, reprinted by permission of Harcourt, Inc. Also in "Four Quartets" in *Collected Poems 1909–1962* by T. S. Eliot, reprinted by permission of Faber and Faber Ltd. and copyright © The Estate.

The paper used in this publication meets the minimum requirements of American National Standard for Information Sciences—Permanence of Paper for Printed Library Materials, ANSI Z39.48–1984.∞™

For a listing of books published and distributed by Syracuse University Press, visit our Web site at SyracuseUniversityPress.syr.edu

ISBN-13: 978-0-8156-0928-5   ISBN-10: 0-8156-0928-0

Library of Congress Cataloging-in-Publication Data
Haven, Stephen.
    The river lock : one boy's life along the Mohawk / Stephen Haven.—1st ed.
    p. cm.
    ISBN 978-0-8156-0928-5 (hardcover : alk. paper) 1. Haven, Stephen—Childhood and youth.
2. Amsterdam (N.Y.)—Biography. 3. Mohawk River Valley (N.Y.)—Biography. I. Title.
    PS3608.A877Z46 2008
    818'.6—dc22
    [B]
    2008002263

Manufactured in the United States of America

In memory of Robert Marshall Haven,
my priest, my father, forever my close friend

———————

For my wife Terri and our new family

———————

For the Koller 49ers

STEPHEN HAVEN is director of the M.F.A. Program in Creative Writing and professor of English at Ashland University, where he also serves as director of the Ashland Poetry Press. He was educated at Amherst College, the University of Iowa, and New York University. He is the author of two poetry collections, *The Long Silence of the Mohawk Carpet Smokestacks* and *Dust and Bread,* and of a chapbook of collaborative translations from contemporary Chinese poetry, *The Enemy in Defensive Positions.* Haven is also editor of *The Poetry of W. D. Snodgrass: Everything Human,* and co-editor of two anthologies of contemporary poetry.

Contents

Illustrations | ix

Author's Note | xi

1. The Mohawk | 1

2. Guy Park | 9

3. Joey and His Tools | 17

4. Sassafras | 26

5. Summer Home | 36

6. Tryon | 50

7. Saratoga Springs | 59

8. Legacy | 72

9. Luisa | 79

10. The Ax | 83

11. PK | 92

12. Bass Line | 102

13. Skully Fags | 106

14. Reading | 113

15. Back in the West End | 119

16. Kamikazes | 125

17. Seder | 133

18. *Five Easy Pieces* | 138

19. Marina and Ray Green | 148

20. The Fly | 157

21. Good Friday | 161

22. Two Dogs | 166

23. Exit 27 | 172

Illustrations

The St. Ann's Episcopal Church
Men and Boys Choir, circa 1964 | *title page*

The Koller 49ers | 6

Luba's Tavern/The Annex | 21

Robert Marshall Haven | 93

Author's Note

Some people appear in this book under fictitious names. Whenever I have substituted a fictitious name for an actual one, I have sustained in the pseudonym the ethnic texture of the original nomenclature.

Many high school friends either do not appear in this book or are underrepresented. Other moments, other stories that in another casting might have belonged to *The River Lock* were finally deleted for the sake of coherence or economy.

Many thanks to Jerry Koller for directing in constructive ways the restless teenage energy he found hanging out on his street corner. Thanks also to Mr. Koller for providing me with a photograph of the Koller 49ers.

Thanks to Glenn Wright, my editor at Syracuse University Press, and to Bob Cowser, Brady Earnhart, Andries and Annabelle Fourie, John Beck, Kathryn Winograd, my wife Terri Haven, and Jim Mendelsohn for their comments and encouragement in various drafting stages of this book.

The River Lock

1

The Mohawk

Some time after I graduated from high school, the Holiday Inn became a Best Western, though I still thought of it as the Holiday. It was Tuesday of Holy Week the day I checked in, three years after missing my twenty-fifth high school reunion. From the fourth floor, the spring-swollen Mohawk was in clear view. I could see, from my room's one window, train tracks bending along one shore. On a side street that ran along the hotel, some municipal employees were sweeping up winter's grit. In the bright shout of their fluorescent vests they worked along the curb, where one last monument of a massive snowbank still sweltered in April's seventy-five degrees.

For some reason, as I lay down to rest from the drive, I thought of how, whenever it snowed, we played tackle football in the road, as if ten inches could cushion the shock of skid marks where the black of the street shone through. Or else we'd play in summer, along the river, on the state-owned Guy Park Manor's one-hundred-yard-long lawn. Then I thought of Paddy Lucas, who I hardly knew. I remembered him mainly for one punt return, and that seemed strange because he or one of his brothers once did something far more outrageous. One of them doused my dog and lit her on fire, so that she rolled and rolled on their lawn, and came home trembling, smelling of charred fur and gasoline. The punt I remembered took an odd bounce and landed in the Mohawk.

Paddy was bigger, tougher than the rest of us—eventually six foot three. He and his family lived a few doors down, both of us in old Victorians, theirs a run-down brick, ours a grey three story. Both garages were carriage houses, built for horses, not cars, ours with an apartment above it. The ball swirled out beyond the lock, toward the center of the dam. His older brothers rode motorcycles—leather or jean jackets, boots, and

1

helmets. The entire family kept a haughty distance. His mother was a nurse. I never knew what his father did for work. Paddy was crazier than any of us and dove right in, in case we doubted him. It had nothing to do with being hot, in mid-July or early August, or with whose ball it was or how much it cost. He didn't give a shit that the open sewer of the river was full of tons of it. Off the floodwall the water was an eight-foot drop.

Years later I ran into his sister in Chinatown. We spotted each other over dinner. She had come to the city for a concert, one rock band or another. I was dating a painter from Cooper Union. That's about all I know of Paddy, the exhaustion of summer burdened with cicadas and the stench of fish, the flash of a moment that sticks, even as it drifts into nothing as we're living it. All these years later, there is still a boy leaping into the filth, into the loveliness of a river, for a ball—just for the hell of it, swimming hard.

I suppose it is the river I remember, though there are dozens of rivers like this one, hundreds of towns. Maybe if the town is small enough, and there is industry, and housing old enough to belong to another century, they all whisper the same thing. If only there are brick-bones and cobblestones that glare through blacktop, and three-family, triple-decker homes, and Victorians gone to seed among the half-razed remnants of the nineteenth century, then the river keeps its own counsel better than any of the men there and speaks its silent sentence. If only I were listening, I thought I might shoo away the dull weight of any single hour, and whatever brought me there, whatever flash of violence once shook me, might breathe with grace and light against the moment's trespass.

Earlier that day, I left my two children with my ex-wife, who was living that year in Rochester, New York, and would pick them up in time to get them home to Ohio for Easter Sunday. I had come back to visit a friend and to spend nearly a week without children, working on the final draft of a book. For most of that afternoon I stared at a laptop. Then I went out to order an early dinner. One brick wall facing the hotel, on the backside of what used to be Trask's Cigar Shop, was completely collapsed. The downtown, on Market and Main, was largely boarded up. A few stray pedestrians wandered into an Italian tailor shop, still open at nearly five o'clock. There was also a take-out pizzeria on the corner welcoming customers, and from all appearances the Key Bank across the street seemed to be doing well, though its doors were closed for the evening. Opposite the hotel lobby, the gothic bell tower of a stone church rose like an ark. My father had been rector there for twenty-eight years.

The next day, when I stopped by the town library to telnet into my office, Mrs. Miller, one of the librarians and widow of my old choirmaster, didn't recognize me. If I chose, I was a stranger among known people, but at least I was embraced by actual things. For the rest of that day I walked unseen by people I had known for the entire lifetime I quit living long ago. Whole buildings, the Chuctanunda Creek, the Mohawk, and even a few trees needed only a silent language to greet me almost by name.

Most of my friends had moved away, though Woody was living nearby, in Fort Hunter, where he had taken his two boys so that they wouldn't have to attend the Amsterdam Public Schools. That night, Woody and I shared an antipasto and then fries and meatball sandwiches, directly across from Guy Park Manor, in Russo's Bar and Grill. We kept to one side, in one of the high-back, wooden booths. As we settled down, a softball team hardscrabbled in after a game, crowding around one table. They started drinking and throwing bills, the kitty going to whoever could guzzle beer fast enough to take the cash.

Though Woody was remarried, he had once been a single father. He described his ex-wife Gina as a pain-in-the-ass type A. She left him for a younger guy and gave him their two children. She always seemed to me as though she should have gone to college, always had her nose in a book—the usual supermarket paperbacks, Danielle Steel and the like—but books, nevertheless, rather than television, even on a Saturday night. Dark-haired Gina was slim and attractive and as sharp-tongued as she was smart.

I hadn't seen Woody in fourteen years. *Sometimes it is better to let the past drift, to wave only a silent hello, or the dull stutter of the present might sink it.* We were both forty-six years old. Woody's hair was still there, a full head compared to my fringe, but thinning, combed straight back.

"I'd rather be dead than red in the head!" I said.

"Fuck you, Harcourt!" he said, both of us laughing.

All the years I was a boy there, almost no one under twenty ever called me Steve or Stephen. Woody is really Mike Weil, six foot even, 220, pale blue eyes, a red head if there ever was one, and though he is half German, the spitting image of a mick. To Woody, everyone had to be something, *Pollack, wop, guinea,* no offense to anyone, *spic, spade, nigger, mick.* But Harcourt is my middle name. From the third grade on, I answered to Harc or Harc-cord, a name so strange that my best friend Frank Johnson permanently tagged it on me. We were the only family in town who drank milk with tea and said *tomaahto* rather than *tomato.*

We talked about a million things. I already knew about Woody's bad shoulder that got him out of the army when he wanted to stay in. I knew also about his brown belt, but he told me again how he had quit heavy lifting and taken up karate "just so I can still take care of myself." Though I had seen him in a number of fights, I also saw him wrap his shirt around some strange boy's bleeding head and flag a car when the boy was without a friend and needed one. Woody had his cheekbone crushed when he was eighteen and I was off at college. He sneaked a six-pack of beer into a South Side bar, where the regulars threw him head first into a pool table. He has a permanent plastic piece where his cheekbone used to be. Woody is a foreman in a welding shop. He used to bench 325.

Woody and I have known each other since we were both nine years old. We played little league baseball together but only became close friends after we were among the decided minority of kids who started sparking up, as we called it, in the tenth grade. In one of my clearest high school memories of Woody, he is eating an ice cream cone. We are walking down Division Street. He takes a lick, gives my dog a lick, takes two for himself, then one for the dog, laughing all the while when I ask him if he's crazy.

"I like dogs, Harc, what can I say?"

Woody has a big heart. He's still friends with his ex-wife's brothers and with the younger guy who took up with Gina. ("What can I do? I knew him since he was a kid. What am I going to do, walk by without saying hello?")

Then there were two seasons on the same basketball team: We took the city league championship in our senior year. Leaner, quicker, I was the playmaker on offense and our top rebounder. Woody was a post-up forward and our biggest scorer. He also had a decent outside shot. Against Tom's Lunch, in the championship game, he had eighteen points and the winning basket. I scored fifteen. Mike Scofield played center. He was a six-foot-one friend from my old Locust Avenue neighborhood whom I had known since I was around three years old, prior to my family's move into our Guy Park Avenue home. Sco and Woody and I were the Koller front line. Mr. Koller, our coach, was a local tax accountant who would take us camping on Mt. Marcy. He was a power weightlifter at some earlier point in his life, a short man with a big barrel chest softening just south of middle age. Mr. K's tax business was located at 49 Lincoln Avenue, kitty corner from Jay Vee's Pizza, where we often spent dull evenings during hot summer months. He had a long, concrete step that led up to his door. When Koller bought the place, he found us sitting there, summer night after summer night. He later told me that rather than trying to fight us, he decided to get involved: He organized us into a basketball team. We were the Koller 49ers. Mr. K would buy us a case of beer when we'd win. He figured we were better off drinking a few indoors with him than out on the street somewhere.

I felt like one of the local professionals—careful, peripheral—as I side-stepped the frenzy of the softball team to find the can. Both bathrooms were directly across from the bar, the men's room small as a linen closet, with one of those gravity-run, wooden toilet tanks overhead. I yanked on the wooden handle of the chain when I was through, rinsed—no soap—and went out to say hello to Michael Leonetti, the dishwasher I once took on, for reasons I can't remember, in one of my rare fights, after a seventh-grade pick-up basketball game. Leonetti, a year younger than me, wouldn't quit, and though I didn't have the stomach for a marathon, I kept knocking him down again and again and he kept getting back up. I think I won that fight, but I took a beating. A punch in the face seemed like less of an emotional experience for Leonetti than it was for me. I remember wishing, as a kid, that my father would hit me every once in a while so it wouldn't be so upsetting when someone else did.

Then, on the way back to the booth, I caught Danny Russo's eye, the bartender and part owner and gifted athlete, my old friend from elementary school. I hadn't seen him in twenty years. Like Leonetti, he was friendly in a polite sort of way—cautious, deferential.

The Koller 49ers, 1975 City League Basketball Champions. Courtesy of Gerard Koller.

"Hello, Harc! How's it going? Hey, welcome home."

Woody and I were on our third beer by the time we talked about Abu, and Maria Luisa's son, and Danny Agresta, and anyone else who was dead. We were taking it a little easy. We stayed away from pitchers, as Woody worked the next day and I wanted to attend the Maundy Thursday morning service at my father's old church. Abu was a half Pole, half Italian whose real name was Mark Reina. I thought of Mark Reina when I first read a Jim Daniels story that begins with the sentence, "Carl Jacks was the kind of guy who got drunk and beat up his own friends." Abu was that sort of guy. He had an epiphany the first time he saw *The Godfather*. He decided never to work again. The movie changed even the way he said his name.

Before long Abu was driving a 1972 Lincoln, affecting a right-off-the-boat Italian accent, and hanging out with kids two and three years younger (and twenty or thirty pounds lighter) than himself. We called him *Abu* because he played basketball, as I once did, in the Protestant church league. The town was just about 99 percent Catholic. My friends took to calling Protestants *Hindus*. From there he became Abu. Just what he was doing, an Italian-Pole in a Lutheran church, I will never know. At six feet, 190, and already out of high school when I was in my sophomore year, he bullied mainly Steven DiBacco into a blood brotherhood that required petty theft as a constant loyalty test. Then it was breaking and entering, fencing stolen jewelry. Once in, there was no getting out again.

Woody never much liked Steven DiBacco. He liked the crazier Abu. But that's another story, and the one that Woody told me that evening had nothing to do with how Abu would pull up in his Lincoln as DiBacco and I walked to school. He'd bark at DiBacco to get in. Once I made the mistake of assuming Abu was picking up both of us. When I opened the back door of his maroon monstrosity, he shot out,

"Anybody talking to you?! Get out of the car!"

"What?"

"Get the fuck out of the car."

All I could think to say was, "Fuck you, Abu!" and then he was chasing me down the hill, threatening to kill me sooner rather than later.

Still another time Abu played Iago to our Othello, on a night when my best friend Frank Johnson and I discovered that our pot was missing. Abu figured Kevin Donovan and Joe Camplone stole it from where we had it hidden. It took five or six beers to convince us to go jump them—Frank and me, primarily, as it was our pot, and a bunch of others to watch. I always felt the absurdity of those situations as though I were acting, as I had never been in more than a handful of fights and really didn't get angry that easily, except in rare moments on the basketball court. I could usually keep quiet, or with the right degree of sarcasm could talk my way out—without losing face—of almost any situation. But there was no getting out of that one.

Abu herded us all into his Lincoln and drove us to the woods where he knew Donovan hung out. We didn't ask any questions. It was almost completely dark. We knew each other from high school. We were friends—not good friends, but friends just the same. When they saw us coming, they had no idea that we were about to attack them. Abu was screaming in my ear when I knocked Camplone down and kicked him in the ribs, the only fight, now that I think of it, that I ever had in high school. Kicked him a few times with the steel toe of a work boot and the top of my foot and realized, right then, how hard it was to get a good kick in. It was like stepping into quicksand—tough to get much power into a kick when you can't follow through. I didn't know enough to stomp him with the heels of my boots. It was enough for Abu. He was jumping up and down as though we had just won the crown.

I ran into Camplone in the tardy line the next school day. I felt something like shame but didn't retract a thing, didn't say a word. I was pretty much sure he didn't do it, but there was no backing out of it then. He scowled at the floor, denied everything, and didn't want to fight again. Camplone had a peach-fuzz black moustache and, like the rest of us, wore jeans and a jean jacket. His dark hair, shoulder length, was parted down the middle. He was probably tougher than me, or at least he scowled better, but he was not quite my size. Maybe he feared my friends. Podowski—a West End kid, a year older than most of us—told me later that Abu was the culprit. He was with him, saw him steal the stash.

But those are other stories. In some minor mode, Francis Ford Coppola might have directed the one that Woody told me over French fries and gravy and two hot meatball sandwiches that night in Russo's Bar and Grill: Crack kicked Abu's ass. They found him dead in the street, thirty-two years old.

2

Guy Park

I suppose it is the river I remember. We lived at 253 Guy Park Avenue, two blocks away. My dog Ishmael—yes, my father, a Melville man, named her Ishmael—used to swim in the Mohawk in the summer and would come back smelling like the dead. My father had a knack for naming dogs. He once attended the same private high school—the Boys' Academy in Albany, New York—that claimed Melville as its most famous alumnus. Our second dog, a lovely German shepherd/St. Bernard mix, became Nemo—no name—when my father couldn't think of what else to call her. Our third dog, Goshen, was a Golden Retriever, named for the land the biblical Joseph gave his brothers after he had forgiven them for selling him into slavery. In some ways we measured our family life by dog age. Ishmael was a mostly shepherd mutt who turned out to be female. Since she was a stray—a wanderer—she became Ishmael, and then Meala once my parents got the gender straight. She died on the day I left for college.

My friends were relentless. Ishmael was a new one on them. They called her Ish. Meala followed me everywhere I went and answered to my call above all others, except on the rare occasion when my mother whistled for her. That dog knew her loyalties. My mother had rescued her from the pound. In those years before leash laws, Meala came and went as she pleased, usually with Frank Johnson and me. She would actually stop at the side of the road and look both ways before crossing, a holdover from her survival days as a stray. Everyone knew her in that town. She had a food route. She would stop by every day for handouts from a dozen housewives. She also never quite got over her habit of raiding the garbage, knocking over metal cans until the lids fell off. Sometimes, too, she'd rip the cardboard caps off glass milk bottles left by the milkman. She'd lick the cream off the top, as far down as her tongue could reach.

My father called her the yellow triangle. When she sat with her snout in the air, her butt formed the base of an isosceles, her nose its one acute angle. She was a small dog but grew so fat that her back was as flat as a table. We rigged a wooden sign that hung from her collar: DO NOT FEED ME—another source of hilarity for my friends. They called her the billboard dog. Meala would forage down to the river to eat dead fish and roll in them. She'd smear them all over her fur. She was gentle with people but fierce with dogs. She would chase squirrels and cats like all get-out, and turn tail and run for her life if anything other than a dog fought back. When she came back with the smell of the Mohawk all over her, my father would send me out to the yard to hook her up to a leash, hose her down, and scrub her with a bar of Ivory.

That was how the river announced its presence in my home, and how we washed it out again. In my early years, the tone my father's church set in our house trumped anything the dog could drag in. My mother threw huge celebrations for Easter, Christmas, Thanksgiving, and Confirmation Day. Every Wednesday in Lent we attended an early evening service, with my father as celebrant, and took part afterward in a Lenten potluck dinner. We could smell the food—tuna and hamburger casseroles, mashed and scalloped potatoes, green beans with chipped almonds, broccoli and cheese—as the half-hour service wound to an end, the entire congregation leaning, by the raised tips of our noses, toward the parish hall and kitchen.

I also loved going to the Men's Breakfast with my brothers and my father. Twice a year, at 6:30 A.M., the men and boys would come to the parish hall for ham and toast and eggs. Those two early Sunday mornings my father would help my brothers and me get ready for church. Otherwise, on any other Sunday of the year, he would be gone for the 8 A.M. service before we were out of bed, leaving my mother to coax the early church-morning chaos of kids into coats and ties and my sister into a Sunday dress. I remember especially my father's hands, how clean and large they were, as he helped my brothers and me with our neckties. I remember drinking out of his cupped palms in our one full bathroom, early in the morning, his thumb the rim from which I sipped.

The house itself, and the way we lived inside of it, gestured toward an earlier era. The fireplace in the living room was deep and graced with blue hunting dogs and deer on white ceramic tile, frozen in a permanent state of harmony and tension. There was a large mahogany staircase in the front hallway and mahogany wainscoting in the dining room. The living room ceiling was nearly ten feet high, the length of the room stretching almost from the front to the back of the house. A lot of reading went on in that room, by my father, my sister, my younger brother and me, my mother tending toward the master bedroom to concentrate on work toward a B.A. and M.A. in psychology from SUNY-Albany. Eventually she finished a Ph.D. from the Union Institute. My older brother practiced his violin in the dining room, where we also kept my mother's upright piano. On Saturdays my brother's scales and arpeggios counted toward his weekly hour's work. The rest of us complained as we vacuumed and mopped.

My father was a genuine unornamented man. He washed his hair for his entire life as his father did, with a bar of soap. Though he claimed he would never force his religious views on us, the ceremonial presence in our home was unavoidable: a blessing at dinner, prayers at bedtime. In high school, it was made clear to me that church attendance was a matter of choice and was not mandatory, though I had to explain myself on the few occasions when I was not scheduled to serve as an acolyte and chose to sleep in after a late Saturday night. How, he asked me, could he encourage other people to bring their children to church when his own son stayed at home? I cared enough about my father's view of things that I didn't have an answer to that question and rarely missed church again.

On Easter we would have a leg of lamb, rubbed with sage and garnished with mint jelly; on Christmas, often, roast beef, mashed potatoes, and Yorkshire pudding. Our neighbor, Helen Heath, the last member of a family that once owned one of the local mills, would often join us, as would a few of the older, widowed members of my father's church—anyone from the parish who would otherwise spend the day alone. Though we never had much money in the family, my mother would polish up the silver, get the fine china out, and spread a linen tablecloth to feed a dozen people, and often many more than that, the men and boys in suits and ties, the women and girls in Sunday bests.

These holiday celebrations began weeks before, in the hymns we sang during choir rehearsal and in all the preparations at home—shopping and cleaning the entire house. Then, on the day itself, we sang before the congregation. My father seemed to find a grace and balance standing on the altar, or in the pulpit, that he did not always carry with him at home or in public. Every service closed with the same blessing, with "the peace that passes understanding." For all those years I lived with my family, those were the words that signaled the end of one celebration and the start of another. At home, after church each Sunday, and all the more so on any church holiday, there were cocktails and beer and wine, crackers and cheese, and then the slow candles and banter of a formal midafternoon meal.

All of this did not take place without a sense of humor. My father loved to tell a good joke, presiding over a well-spread table. Many of his most raunchy jokes came from the diocesan ministers' annual convention, where Anglican priests unleashed on each other some of the repressed scatological humor they could never share with their parishioners. My father would restrain himself if we had guests in our home, but both barrels were open and firing if we were celebrating with immediate family only.

The jokes that came out of that annual conference weren't likely to stand up to any PC litmus test. My father particularly enjoyed telling these jokes when my grandmother, my mother's mother, was seated at the table. My grandmother sometimes wore long white gloves on formal occasions and made a big deal out of her married name. She thought Harcourt was aristocratic in origin, despite my grandfather's compromised circumstance when he lost re-election for town judge in Poughkeepsie, New York, and then failed to establish a lucrative law practice in Albany. Haven, in my grandmother's opinion, was a common name. My father found this amusing. He would wait until my mother disappeared into the kitchen, then lay in on my grandmother, though only indirectly, through humor. One of the jokes he often told was about an Orthodox rabbi and a Catholic priest traveling back together by train from their respective clerical conventions in Chicago. The priest says to the rabbi, "Tell me, Rabbi, aren't you ever tempted, when you are away from your congregation, to violate your dietary restrictions?"

"Yes, Father, I confess to you, and to no one else, that while I was away, over the past weekend, I sneaked into a deli and placed onto my dry tongue a small piece of pork, and then could stand it no longer and ordered a ham sandwich.

"But Father," the rabbi continues, "now that we are being so honest with one another, have you never, when you are away from your home parish, been tempted to commit a sin of the flesh?"

"Okay, Rabbi, yes, I confess, last Friday, when the other priests returned to their rooms in the evening, I slipped out of the hotel and offered, much to my shame, the sanctity of my vows and my virginity to a prostitute!"

The rabbi looks at the priest, the priest at the rabbi. There is an awkward moment of silence, then the rabbi says, "Sure beats the hell out of ham, doesn't it, Father?!"

Grandmother Harcourt would scowl and shake her head. Grandmother Haven, if she were present, would look out the window and say, "My, has anyone noticed how beautiful the trees are today? What a lovely spring we've been having!" My brothers and I would howl with laughter no matter that we had heard the joke many times before.

The clincher, the joke that was sure to send Grandmother Harcourt flying for cover to the bathroom, the kitchen, or the bedroom at the top of the back stairs where she usually slept when she visited, was the one about the man who suffered a broken jaw and had his mouth wired shut. The doctors approached him about the possibility of being fed in an experimental way that would allow for something other than a liquid diet. My father would clench his teeth together as he spoke the man's lines.

"What exactly do you have in mind?"

"Well, we thought we would try to feed you rectally."

"Rectally!?" My father's eyes bulged in mock horror, his grimace revealing his clenched teeth whenever he spoke the patient's lines. When he spoke as the doctor, he was calm and businesslike:

"Yes, well, what would you like for dinner?"

"I think I'll have a little steak," the man grimaced, "medium rare, with a baked potato, sour cream and butter both, green beans, apple pie, and black coffee for dessert."

The nurse comes in and sticks the steak up inside him. The man groans a little. Then the doctor asks him, "How are you doing there, guy?"

"Just fine!" the man replies. "I think I'm fine." Then the nurse goes ahead and rams the potato in, followed by the green beans. The man grunts again.

"Do you think you might have room for a little dessert?" the doctor asks.

"Sure!" the man replies. The nurse slips the apple pie up inside of him. Then she pours the black coffee in. The man screams like there's no tomorrow.

"What's the matter?" the doctor asks, "What's the matter? Is it too hot?"

"No!" the man replies, "it's too sweet!"

My father was his own best audience, laughing all the way through. No one could quite deliver that joke as he did, though I tried, on one occasion, to tell it to one of my closest college friends and received in return only a paternalistic, impatient grin.

After sitting through that joke a few times, Grandmother Harcourt would excuse herself from the room whenever she heard my father slip into the opening line. Standing at the head of the dining room table, carving away at a baked ham, roast turkey, roast beef, or leg of lamb, a fire in the living room, my father would laugh and we laughed with him as my grandmother frowned off, though we loved her, too. Once, after he had just baptized my sister's youngest child, after his own mother had already died, my father carried that new life up and down the aisles of our packed church, then walked up to the pew where my grandmother was standing and, poised and balanced as he always was before a congregation, placed the baby in her arms.

Most of my friends didn't quite know what to make of my family. My mother had studied voice during the two years she spent at Smith College and would sing her operatic Italian in a way that didn't quite sound like home to the local sons and grandsons of Sicily and southern Italy. Once, in a friend's home when I was in the third grade, an old man pulled out an old accordion and my friend's mother began to sing. I sure didn't feel like a natural part of that domestic scene. It must have been somewhat that way in my home for many of my friends. Joe Battaglia, our diminutive playground point guard, who could dribble and pass well but had a tough time getting off a shot, broke up laughing on one of the few occasions he heard my mother sing. I remember responding in a similar way, though more with impatience than humor, the first time I heard Beijing Opera—a nasal, pentatonic vibrato that just about cleaned out my sinuses. It must have been something like that for Joe Battag, a kind of music he had never encountered before, my mother singing Verdi in the kitchen, my brother practicing his violin in the dining room.

Frank Johnson, having squatter's rights from the third grade on, was probably the only one of my friends who was ever really comfortable in my home, though Donny Overbaugh, during junior high school, also spent a lot of time there. OB and I would shut the door to my room for a little privacy. My father would come up the front stairs quietly and throw the door suddenly open.

"What's going on in here, Stephen? We have an Open Door Policy in this home. An Open Door Policy!" he would say before leaving the door cracked and heading back downstairs. That was another source of humor for my friends, as Donny O reported it to them, our own local version of nineteenth-century world history.

After high school, when I was home from college, my father would interrogate Woody whenever he came over.

"So, Woody, what are you up to these days? What are you doing with yourself?" my father would ask in his formal baritone. "What are your plans for the future?"

Woody felt as though he were being interviewed and would always pretty much say the same thing:

"I am a working man. I work every day. I'm a metal banger. It's always the same thing. I work," as if he were tired of answering always the same question. My father was not impressed that Woody was a welder and that he had so little to say for himself.

"What's wrong with your father, Harc?" Woody asked me one day, after we left my house. "Your old man's a trip! Why is he so serious?"

"He's not serious, Wood, he's just saying hello. That's all he's doing. He's just saying hi."

"He acts like somebody died, or something."

"That's just his way, Wood. He's just trying to be friendly."

"Yeah, well, he acts like I killed somebody."

As I mixed wine with water, helped my father bless the bread, sang throughout my childhood in the church choir, and didn't so much celebrate the church seasons as breathe in them, I learned from my father, despite any contradiction, at least something of what Walt Whitman later taught me: "There is in the possession of . . . each single individual, something so transcendent, so incapable of gradations that . . . it places all beings on a common level, utterly regardless of the distinctions of intellect, virtue, station, or any height or lowliness whatever." Though I sometimes saw my father fail the spirit of that understanding, I saw him embody it, too, in and outside of the church. I saw it in the pregnant teenagers who came to live in our house until they gave birth to their children, then gave them up for adoption and could return to their home towns. I saw it in the widow Mrs. Wilcox, who my father repeatedly invited over to our house for dinner. I heard it in her Hungarian accent, tasted it in her relentless barrage of fruitcakes, and felt it in her hands as she squeezed my cheek with her thumb and index finger, or lightly patted both sides of my face, her own cheeks veritable powder kegs doused with an overdose of rouge.

Yet Woody would have occupied only the most awkward place at my parents' dining room table if he had ever been offered one. Maybe my father was not comfortable with what he saw in Woody—the macho man. Maybe my father couldn't see the good-spirit gravitas in Woody beyond his "more-than-glad-to-kick-your-ass" exterior.

My father would drive Jeffrey Teabout's mother 120 miles to visit her son in prison, yet would not entertain her as a guest in his home.

"Ourself behind ourself, concealed," as Emily Dickinson says, as if the self were both plural and singular, layers overlapping layers, and all selves shared something in common, were all singular parts of some plural pronoun.

Years later, when I told my parents that I planned to marry a mainland Chinese girl, my father was deeply and quietly skeptical, with good reason as it turned out, though he hadn't met her yet. My mother poured herself a whiskey and lit up a cigarette. She hadn't smoked in years.

3

Joey and His Tools

"The town's gone to the Ricans, Harc!" Or so Woody claimed that night in Russo's Bar and Grill. I noticed the change earlier that day when I tried to catch lunch at Lorenzo's, in Woody's old neighborhood, corner of Union and Garden, where Woody's younger brother Tom used to work as a cook. I parked my car and walked past double and triple deckers, two- and three-family homes. Little oxygen masks of grass graced some of the lots, though most of the houses were built right up to the sidewalk. The houses were constructed in the twenties by the owners of the Mohawk Mills, then sold or leased to their workers. The street was intensely blacktop and concrete. For as long as I was in touch with the Amsterdam crowd, Woody's brother worked at Lorenzo's. I never felt right calling him Worm, as everyone else did, I guess because he was, unlike Woody, so skinny and not very strong: little brother, blond hair, clearly his mother's child.

As I remember him, Tom was always wearing a white, full-length apron. He would come out of the kitchen, glad to see me, always grinning. He called me Harc, like everyone else. I called him Tom. I knew that Tom's employers, the Lanzi family, owners of Lorenzo's, had done so well with the corner restaurant that they bought a resort establishment on the lower part of the Great Sacandaga Lake and changed the name to Lanzis on the Lake. I thought they might have also kept the old restaurant going, opposite corner to the house where Woody and his brother and sister were raised by their father (Woody's mother died young in a car crash). I tried Lorenzo's locked door. A Puerto Rican mother and a couple of young teenagers eyed me suspiciously from Woody's old porch. The houses, always in a state of general disrepair, seemed worse now: fallen porches, loose boards, some missing patches of fake-brick siding—a throwback to the days before aluminum or vinyl.

17

Somewhere around the fall of my sophomore year, Frank Johnson and I wandered down from the West End to hang out with Woody and his buddies in Brooks's basement apartment, two blocks away from Woody's house. We'd order take-out grinders and steak sandwiches from Lorenzo's and chip in to buy cases of beer for Fridays and Saturdays, and kegs for bigger weekends. I still remember Woody, up on a stool, doing his Jimi Hendrix "Purple Haze" thing with a broom. Joe Murphy was Woody's best friend, a skinny Irish kid—otherwise known as Murph, or J.T., or Joey Tools, or Joey and his Tools, for all his fooling around with stereos and speakers and other things, taking them apart and putting them back together again. He lived two doors down from Lorenzo's, one door from The Annex. The Annex was formerly Luba's Tavern, a basement pub big enough for a bar and a pool table, a jukebox and not much else. When the Lanzi family bought Luba's Tavern, they changed its name to The Annex, as if it were an extension of the family restaurant on the corner.

There were essentially five of us in our main high school party group—Murph, Woody, Frank, Rod Stanavich, and me. Frank and I were from the West End, Woody and Murph from Union Street, Rod from Pollack Hill. We teamed up with a group a year younger than us, also from the Union Street neighborhood, mainly because one of them—Brooks—had a warm place to party during the long upstate New York winter months.

Murph was more or less the center of that Union Street group. He was one of the most carefree guys I have ever known. We used to walk to his house during our school lunch period to smoke a joint or two. Murph lived in a railroad flat, with his parents and one of his two brothers, on the second floor of a two-family home. The door opened into the living room where a gas stove generated enough heat for the entire place. His parents' bedroom was off to the right, on the way in—a room large enough for a dresser and a double bed. There were two other bedrooms in the flat and a walk-through kitchen, with a narrow table against one wall, chairs at either end. We had about fifteen minutes of the lunch break to smoke the pot and share my brown bag and whatever else Murph could dig up from his refrigerator. Murph's method of doing the dishes was to hold a plate by its edge under running water. He'd do the same with glasses, dabbing at some spots with a rag, but basically just rinsing them off. As he repeatedly showed me, even peanut butter rinses off if you hold it under the faucet long enough.

It didn't matter that Murph was easily the weakest kid his age in the Union Street crowd. He was the sort of guy who always seemed to be having the absolute time of his life, no matter the company. That meant the rest of the Union Street kids listened to him. Murph had street smarts, and gadget smarts, too, though he once told me that he would never write to me—no offense—when I headed off to college, as he couldn't put a few good sentences together, much less an entire letter, and was embarrassed even to try. He liked to wear a big baggy brown coat—probably his older brother's—and browse in music stores, where he'd line up some albums, slip his zipped coat over them, and then walk out, one hand in his pocket, keeping the albums where he wanted them (headed in the direction of his bedroom collection), the other hand hanging, as if to assure the music store owner that everything was casually cool. The more stuff Murph got away with, the more we expected of him, though we all waited for his luck to break.

One time, out of sheer boredom, Murph, Woody, and I borrowed my younger brother's BB gun and minibike and decided to hunt each other in the woods. We put two of us on the bike and one in the woods with the gun. The minibike could barely do 35 mph with a half-grown teenager riding solo. With Woody and me on board, it sputtered uphill. Murph ran alongside, laughing like crazy, cocking the gun as many times as he could, pumping me full of BBs through my colored T-shirt. Our one rule was that you couldn't shoot above the neck. My brother Tom wasn't too pleased when we crashed the bike and ripped the fuel line. His turn with the gun, Woody had hidden behind a tree, then jumped out head on and aimed at my chest a few feet away. I turned the wheel sharp and the whole thing went over. That was our idea of a good time. We laughed and laughed.

Another time Murph decided he wanted to learn bass guitar and simply walked into the local music store, looked around for a minute, then grabbed the bass from the display window nearest the door and sprinted the five blocks home. The owner of the music store was a parishioner in my father's church. In still another adventure, Murph was dating a girl who lived in Watertown, a good sixty miles away from Amsterdam. He met her at a Who concert at SPA—the Saratoga Performing Arts Center. He couldn't let a little transportation impede a sure chance to get laid. He started "borrowing" cars off the street. I don't know if he found the keys in them or hot-wired them. He would take one for the night and return it in the morning, if not exactly to where it had been, then to somewhere close by. He figured the police wouldn't be so worried about catching him if everyone got their cars back.

The Annex was Murph's good neighbor, the door to his house only a few feet from the concrete stairs leading down to the basement pub. The Annex was geared toward high school and slightly older kids. Eddie Witek had his face cut there, simply for being from elsewhere. In a sprawling metropolis of twenty thousand or so people, elsewhere was a couple miles down the road. The South Side kids didn't hang out in Union Street bars and vice versa. The regulars held Witek down and scarred his cheeks with a broken bottle. That happened the year after I left for college. Witek once played basketball and baseball for the high school. I saw him in The Annex at least a couple of times. For a few years, since I knew the kids in the neighborhood, and since the Lanzi family owned the bar and Larry Lanzi played basketball with me on the Koller 49ers, I was in. Though I never really looked my age, I could get a drink there from the time I was fifteen. All I had to do was slap a quarter on the bar. I remember coming home from college and pulling up in a snowstorm, in my father's Toyota Corolla, while Murph, catching sight of me from the other side of the Budweiser Beer sign, shouted from the door, "Blow it out your ass, Haven!"—shit-eating grin, a beer, one of them for me, in each hand.

Some ten years later, when Larry Lanzi's little brother had grown up and didn't know me from Adam, The Annex taught me more about never going home again than I ever learned at Amherst College. On the day my hometown celebrated its centennial anniversary, I was in the middle of a residency at Yaddo, an artists' colony in Saratoga Springs, New York, thirty miles north of Amsterdam on Route 67. I spent some days foraging around Amsterdam with Fern, a black photographer from New York City, and then came back for the centennial celebration. I eventually wrote that summer a whole series of poems about Amsterdam. My family was still

Luba's Tavern/The Annex, circa 1985. Courtesy of the author.

living on Guy Park Avenue. Kirk Douglass, our most famous native son, stood in an open car at the head of the centennial parade, throwing roses to septua- and octogenarians.

Toward the end of the day, I ran into Steven DiBacco. He wanted me to meet him for a drink at The Annex. I told him I would see him there later, as Woody and his wife Gina—they were still married then—had invited me over to their trailer for dinner. By the time I got to The Annex, Steven was drunk and all coked out, face down on the bar. I didn't know anyone else there except for the bartender, who I remembered as a ten-year-old kid. He didn't know me, or else he did and smelled college on me or some kind of fun. The bar was packed. It was all I could do to stay clear of the pool table.

I ordered a beer and stuck with DiBacco, standing near his barstool, though he could barely raise his head to say *Har-COURT!* There was a stocky guy playing pool, five feet ten or so. He came around to my side of the table, backed away to line up his shot, and caught me, as if by accident, hard in the ribs with the butt of his stick. Next it was a shot to my gut with his elbow as he came around the table to his drink at the bar. I moved to the other side of DiBacco's stool. The bartender, the Lanzi kid, came around the bar laughing and shouting something I didn't understand. He grabbed the stocky kid from behind, grinned, and shouted again, then stomped on my foot as he released his bear hug. I knew, right then, that the door would slam in a minute or so and found my way to the car.

Woody later told me I was lucky to get out of The Annex that night. He knew exactly who this guy was: He had paratrooped into Granada. He would have gladly—professionally—dismembered me, quickly at first, then more slowly. Gina called him a kid.

"He's not a kid, Gina. He's twenty-one. Who you calling a kid? Once you're twenty-one, you're not a kid anymore."

"He's still a kid, Woody. He's a kid to me."

I took it personally. The town, the bar, spat me out, right in the middle of its centennial celebration! I suppose I am stubborn enough that the more the town wanted rid of me, the more I wanted to understand my own strange presence there, as it floated through my childhood, in the bars, in my father's church, in the company of my high school friends. Woody and Gina told me never to go back to The Annex again.

One high school August night, on our way home from drinking in the baseball fields, a group of us was cutting through the high school grounds, the break-off point where the Union Street kids would turn four blocks east. Those of us who lived in the West End, on Guy Park or Division or Stewart Street—Frank and me and Steven DiBacco—usually headed the other way, six blocks west. By then Murph was working as a cook at the Holiday Inn. I was pumping gas on the New York State Thruway. Murph was bothered that night by the fact that there were "two big sucking speakers" mounted some twenty feet up in the high school auditorium. He had long been eyeing them. They were right down the hall. That's how close they were. I don't remember exactly who was there as we walked by the dark green, double glass doors on the side of the school. What I remember is Murph wanting to know who was a chickenshit and who was coming in "right fucking now!" That the police made regular rounds through the high school parking lot, their cruisers sliding along the back of the school almost every hour, actually fed Murph's bravado. "They'll never even fucking know!"

When Murph lifted a metal garbage can over his head and threw it through the door, I was leaning heavily toward college. I was just over a year away. I left them to walk the half mile back to the West End and heard all about it later. Murph found the high school's twenty-foot stepladder, got the speakers down, hid them in the football stadium's concession stand, and came back two days later to pick them up in someone's van. He cut the speakers out, made new boxes for them, and laughed about it for weeks.

Murph was always busting someone's ass or finding some reason for everyone to laugh. He had a big head of dirty-blond hair, curly and thick as an afro, and at five foot ten weighed all of about 130 pounds. He decided, spontaneously one night, that there was just about nothing better than "tits," and soon everyone was saying it. A brand new 1973 Camaro was tits. So was the latest *Planet of the Apes* film. So was a good fight, though Murph wasn't a fighter, or a good concert, Kiss or Led Zeppelin or Aerosmith, or a kick-ass bag of dope. A girl who had not yet developed physically was a "sprouter" in Murph's anatomical nomenclature. He was just about the worst athlete I'd ever seen, but he had somewhat of an athletic arrogance about him—a swagger, not without laughter, a constant assumption that he was in control, or was about to be.

Though Murph was never caught stealing anything, he eventually spent twelve weekends in jail for selling pot to a New York State undercover drug-enforcement officer—the Man-Lady, as we called her. We laughed about how Murph would sell weed to anyone—only small-time stuff, enough to pay for his own smoke. He would take an ounce of pot, split it into three bags, fluff up a third of it, sell it for a half, and do it again. We called him the fluffer nutter. Then a tough woman moved to Amsterdam and started wearing—no joke—a fake moustache around town. That's how she came to be the Man-Lady. Most of us wouldn't go near her jean jacket and storm-trooper boots—the exaggerated swagger of a grown teenager a little shy on testosterone. Murph let her in to his parents' apartment when they were at work and smoked a joint or two with her. He sold her a light half ounce.

Maybe cheating the Man-Lady out of a full sixty-four grams saved Murph from real time in a state prison, though where they sent him, to the Fulton County jail, was real enough. By the time he was arrested, his job at the Holiday Inn had become full time, weekdays, so the judge took some kind of mercy on him: He gave him "youthful offender status" and twelve weekends in jail, rather than twenty-four days running. I had been in the Fulton County jail before, at Christmas time, when my father would bring the prisoners Communion. Someone would play an autoharp while we sang Christmas hymns, a few of the prisoners joining in, a few of them glaring at me, threatening. The Fulton County jail was a holding pen for anyone who couldn't afford bail, and for convicted prisoners waiting to be transferred to medium- and maximum-security prisons. It was old and dark. There were no nets on the hoops of the outdoor basketball courts.

Fulton County jail was rough on Murph. Since he was in and out every weekend, the other guys expected him to smuggle in drugs. The options weren't pretty. Just before five o'clock on a Friday, when Murph got ready to go in, he would pop as many downs as he thought he could handle and sleep a full forty-eight hours until they let him out again.

Murph's love of music saved his ass from the mills or from some other sort of low-paying job in Amsterdam: He joined Bobby Boyer's band. He couldn't play a lick on the electric bass, but he figured out how to wire lights, rig a sound system, and he didn't mind driving the band's van. Bobby Boyer used to take his band on the road to Burlington, Vermont. That's where Murph ended up.

A few nights before my first wedding, Murph was doing lines of coke off the bar. He told me he had a good desk job in Burlington. He started looking over the shoulder of a guy at work who ran the computer for his company's loading dock, then talked his way into the job when the man quit. The computer was in an air-conditioned office. Murph worked third shift. One hundred percent of the air was filtered every six minutes, which meant he could smoke a joint right at his desk in the early morning when no one was around. No one ever knew the difference.

Murph loved the people he worked with, too, though they thought he got carried away when in the spirit of the moment he jumped up on a table, unbuckled his belt, and mooned them at their last Christmas party. So he told me that night before my first wedding. Still, Murph never quite seemed to go overboard, at least in my view of things. Despite all the risks he took, he always seemed to land on his feet. His parents both worked in one of the mills and didn't own a car, so money was never even there. One way or another, Murph was going to spark a party, and he only once got caught on the wrong side of the law.

When I think of Murph, he's down in Brooks's basement late on a Saturday night, sucking on a cigarette, commandeering the turntable, beer in hand—*don't touch it, don't even think about it!* The same side of the same Aerosmith album, over and over again. I thought I would go brain dead. An obsession matched only by my father's love of Beethoven and Bach, the violin concerto, the flute sonatas. Only those two albums ground into our heads, each slow Sunday afternoon, until, even within such a limited classical repertoire, I understood what passion was. To this day I can whistle whole movements by heart.

4

Sassafras

Woody and I left Russo's that Wednesday night with half the softball team still gathered around one center table. We slipped out the side door to the parking lot and drove in separate cars to the Best Western for a nightcap. The bartender served us each a beer and told us to take our time. It was after 10 P.M., a weekday night, and no one else was there. The lounge had a 1970s disco decor with mirrors, red booths, soft lighting, and herds of stallions silk-screened on some of the walls. We stuck to the bar. It was only then we started laughing about Frank.

Though Frank was only about five foot nine, you didn't want to get in a battle with him, even if you were tougher and stronger. You would have to knock him into the hospital or it would never end. Frank was sensitive, passionate, easily offended, and loyal to the last man. A certain smirk in his eye lent a sweetness to his swagger that stayed with him even to the edge of anger. Friendship with Frank was a permanent state of being. You were either in or out of that state. I was permanently in. We trusted each other like brothers. Until Frank reached puberty, I could more than hold my own in our puppy tangles. But he started lifting weights when he was twelve and never quit. One spring day toward the end of sixth grade, he pinned me. Before long, he was boxing and sprouted Popeye forearms.

Frank's real name was John Franklin Johnson. Everyone in his family called him Frank. He was John Franklin Emerick before his mother re-married, sometime before I met him in the third grade. I told Woody my story of going to visit Frank in South Carolina, when I was teaching at Baylor University. I jogged way out of my way on a drive from New York to Texas to see him. Frank was married by then, stationed in Charlotte, home port of his ship, the USS *Kitty Hawk*. We laughed about his first fight in the navy. When they called roll they called his legal name: John. He had

26

Frank tattooed on one forearm. He swung at the first guy who wanted to know who his boyfriend was.

Woody's one complaint about Frank was that he would never phone him from Indian Lake when visiting his parents in the Adirondacks. They moved there just before his senior year in high school. Or Frank would call to say that he was coming into town and wouldn't show. Or Woody would give him a ring in South Carolina and Frank would say he'd call him right back, and then Woody wouldn't hear. "Fuckin' Frankie," was where Woody left it, not without affection. We made plans to get together again on the last night before I left Amsterdam. Then I took the elevator up to bed.

If there was one thing Frank's mother cared about, it was eating together as a family at 4:30 in the afternoon, summer, spring, and autumn, as soon as Mr. Johnson drove home from work. In every season but winter, he worked construction in Glens Falls, an hour north of Amsterdam. Mrs. Johnson was a redhead, like her oldest son Billy, and the life force of the Johnson home. She had a quick smile and seemed—for what my mother told me of such things—to have a southern personality. She was a big woman who would sometimes slim down on one diet or another and then get big again. There were five kids and two parents squeezed around the kitchen table those late afternoons—Frank and his brother Billy, his older sister Barbara, two younger half-brothers, and baby Amy in the playpen. When the Johnson boys got older, only football or wrestling practice gave them a pass from a seat at that afternoon family gathering. Sometimes I pulled a chair up to their table, the seventh kid. Behind his back, Frank and Billy called their stepfather Doug or Douglass. He would knock them around from time to time, until Billy got old and big enough to hit him back.

The Johnsons lived in a railroad flat, one block down from our Victorian row. In elementary school, there were no money differences between Frank and me. We shared whatever money we could make by lawn mowing, snow shoveling, or canvassing housewives in the neighborhood for the bottle-clutter of their basements, kitchens, or screened porches. We were best friends in the way only children can be, with an unconditional commitment to one another that gained in intensity what it lost in longevity, stronger during those school years even than our loyalty to our actual brothers. Summers when I slept over at Frank's house, Billy slept out on the back porch. I took Billy's spot in the Johnson brothers' double bed.

It was through Mary's influence that her oldest son had his drive and Frank his easily offended pride, and both of them their deep-bellied laughter. Mary seemed to take in stride all of Billy's success—eventual captain of the high school football team, president of his class, Albany area wrestling champ, a solid B+ GPA. As a senior in high school, Billy bolstered the defensive line with a fervor and a weight-lifting regimen that packed in him a punch disproportionate to his size. He was six feet even, 185 pounds. Maybe that's what it takes to make a genuine football player—a powerful throttle opened and reigned in by discipline.

Billy seemed to lead the charmed adolescent life of a lucky man. He had conventional success and he broke the rules. That made him more or less a model for both Frank and me, and a hard act to follow. But if Mary Johnson was proud of her oldest son, no child of hers played second fiddle to any other. She was as much in Frank's corner as she was in Billy's, though Frank struggled in school and was constantly getting into trouble. Even Mary got a laugh out of Frank when he would say "mazagine" instead of "magazine" and spelled it that way. Until the sixth grade he wrote backward tails on his *j*'s, *y*'s, and *g*'s.

I met Frank on one of my first days at the Guy Park Avenue Elementary School, under the careful eye of Miss Hoos, our severe third-grade teacher. On recess duty that day, beneath a grey hive of cotton-candy hair, she watched as Frank scissored together the middle and index fingers of his two hands and said, "Hi, I'm John Johnson. It kind of fits together." I called him John until I figured out that the rest of his family called him Frank. From that point on, we walked together every day to face Miss Hoos.

Frank's love, without malice, of an irreverent act, his utter disregard for any trouble he might get into, was a kind of charisma in him, or its near approximation. He insisted on drawing a smiley on anything he turned in for art class, long before the icon for "have a nice day" came into its own as a national cliché. The art teacher couldn't understand why Frank would ruin perfectly good drawings. We'd be asked to draw a Halloween cat, and there on the black of its raised fur Frank's round, white face grinned at her. As soon as she cornered him to talk about it, he claimed it as his mark—a manifesto of sorts. A smiley on all art projects became his personal policy, despite what the teacher thought about it—a jack-o-lantern's leer on the American flag or nestled in among the colored eggs of spring. It was as if Frank got a laugh out of whatever activity might most fully undermine his own best interests.

Then a new school opened at the beginning of fourth grade: Clara S. Bacon Elementary, exactly nine-tenths of a steep mile up Henrietta Boulevard. We walked in all kinds of weather, though it is winter I remember most. On our way home from school, the thud of our wet snowballs kettle-drummed against empty diesel trailers (a flat, less resonant thud meant a full load). Then the sharp hiss of air brakes, the trucker's anger while we watched from a safe distance, halfway up Henrietta's wooded hills. From there we went to cars. The truck drivers were usually too busy to chase us. They would swear and threaten to kick our asses but wouldn't often leave their rigs. We weren't as much interested in scaring drivers with our light shock bombs splashing on their windshields. We wanted to be chased. Or rather, Frank wanted to be, and I went along, at first reluctantly.

Only some of the younger drivers seemed to be game in running after us through "the springs"—the fields and glen behind Bacon School, to which we often escaped. We knew those woods well. The spring was fed by the Sassafras Creek. The main path followed the creek for a couple of miles through the Sassafras Woods then opened to the fourth hole of the Municipal Golf Course. There were stairs built into the wooded hills, leading back up to the elementary school and to the baseball diamond behind it. Sometimes on the way home we cut out the bottoms and sides of large cardboard boxes and used them to go sledding. When I started to take cello lessons in school, we would slide my cello ahead and follow down on the cardboard. That cello made more than its share of crash landings. Quite a few of my lessons involved Mr. Barnello, the string teacher, operating on the instrument with a large tube of Elmer's glue.

No telling what those teenage drivers might have done if they had actually caught one of us. I can only imagine Frank's shocked outrage, as if he were the victim, if one of them had caught him red-handed and dragged him to his car. Frank showed no fear in almost any situation, though his glee would instantly turn to outrage whenever he was physically confronted. I had seen that transition in him when his brother Billy occasionally knocked him around or threw a ball at him after the Johnson boys teamed up and lost a pick-up game. Unlike Frank, I was terrified whenever we went bombing at the possibility of being caught, shamed before my parents. Still, it was too strong for me: the thrill of the chase, the safe slide into home, hanging our sweat-soaked hats and saturated gloves on the forced-steam radiator in my room, the cheer of co-conspirators as we crossed the line, adventured out, and made it back to our regular selves.

After awhile it wasn't enough to bomb moving vehicles; we started picking on "The Guy." The Guy had a spring water business on the steepest part of Henrietta. It was a little one-room affair, complete with a shingle roof and a metal chimney—the only house on that side of the forested street. He would deliver spring water in five-gallon jugs on the back of a pickup. At first we simply went after his truck when he drove past. The Guy knew the paths into the woods as well as we did, as he'd sometimes watch us disappear into one of them, and then we'd find him waiting on the other side. That would force us back in the direction of school. We used to split up when The Guy chased us so that he would have to choose.

One time he chose me—cornered me into a large field, right next to the Sassafras Woods. I was so tired from running that I sat down in the snow, some fifty feet from where he parked. The Guy got out of his truck, in his blue coveralls and work boots, red flannel vest and cap, and just stood there watching me. He must have been sixty. I was too exhausted to run anymore, though I would have found my second wind and easily side-stepped him had he walked into the field to come after me. Frank was already home free. The sun was low in the sky, one of those December late-afternoon upstate New York dusks, when spring is a lifetime off and death is in the air. Our school let out at 3 P.M. It must have been after four o'clock by then. The Guy was standing between me and my old identity—the good kid. Between me and my dinner and a dry set of clothes. I sat there in the snow watching him watch me. It seemed to last forever. Eventually he tired of waiting, got back into his truck, and let me go.

We tortured The Guy for three elementary school years. We had his goat. The Guy was always an option in winter. We started walking right up to his spring-water hut, throwing snowballs at his parked truck. We didn't even wait for him to drive by. We could see him watching us from his one window. He was always game. He'd fly out the door. I later found out that he was the uncle of the Robertsons, a family in my father's church. That gave me pause to think.

But mainly we played board games on those winter school afternoons— chess, Monopoly, Stratego, Life, Careers, and a Milton Bradley World War I game called Dog Fight. If Frank was tougher than me by the spring of sixth grade, I had the upper hand in board games. I was merciless with him, but he had the sort of competitive edge that persuaded him to believe that he would win every next game. He was always ready to set the pieces up again. In chess, with the exception of one or two games, I beat him every time we played. Eventually, when we were in seventh grade, I took second place in a citywide chess tournament. Frank brought to those chess games the same sort of attitude he later brought into the boxing ring. He refused to give up. The past had nothing to do with it. The next round was sure to be his lucky strike.

Frank fared better in Monopoly. He won at least a good cutthroat share of those games. Still, I knew from experience that the odds were higher for winning Monopoly if you bought the Oranges first—New York, St. James, and Tennessee—rather than the more expensive Reds, Yellows, or Greens. The way we played, we dealt all the properties out, negotiated a trade that would give us each a monopoly or two, and then let the dice decide the game. I always held out for the Oranges. Frank almost always built first on Pacific, North Carolina, and Pennsylvania, where houses were two hundred dollars each. I figured out early that we were cash poor at the beginning of the game. To build houses and hotels quickly you needed cheaper property. Also, a player didn't always make it all the way around the board. *Go To Jail* or *Chance* or *Community Chest* could send you skipping past *Go*, past the knockout punch of the imperial Greens. The Oranges were a more modest, regular payday. It was a strategy that worked at least more than half the time. Even to this day my brothers and sister feel at least a degree of disgust with me at the way I played those board games. We played the way Frank would later play football, or I would play basketball. We wanted to knock someone's head off. Frank and I were on the same page. We played to win.

Whatever impact I may have had on Frank's character, he counterbalanced at least one thing in me: my parents' expectations that I would behave. Frank was looking out for me. Even though I was bigger than most of the kids in my grade, I couldn't afford, in Frank's opinion, to be known as a wimp. That meant I had to fight someone. Until Frank started lifting weights, until the other boys got their junior high growth spurts before I got mine, there were only two kids in my class who could take me—Paglietta and Gutowski. At first everyone assumed that Danny Russo was number three. The utter logic of events my fourth- or fifth-grade year led to my one fight with Danny Russo. I remember standing in my kitchen one morning, during one of our first years in our new house, and telling my mother that I was out to make a good reputation. She praised me. She didn't know that meant I could no longer stand out as different. It meant that I had to keep my mouth shut when things went wrong, in or after school. It meant I had to fight Danny Russo.

The fights at Bacon Elementary were nothing compared to the fights at many of the other schools in Amsterdam. One rule at Bacon was that there were no punches to the head. Bruno Paglietta—Pags—presided over the whole thing. He gave us a choice between a pin and a cry. We chose a cry—the first one of us to shed a tear would lose. Russo went on to be a varsity basketball player and quarterback for the high school junior varsity team. He was a good kid. I had no reason to fight him. I got him in a scissor lock and squeezed the hell out of his stomach. Then I squeezed the hell out of his head and gave him a noogie to boot. He started to cry. That ranked me as number three, until Donny Overbaugh arrived.

The day Overbaugh showed up at Clara S. Bacon, the power balance in the school shifted irreparably. I first became aware of him in the cafeteria. He was sitting directly across from me, flicking spilled kernels of corn off the table with his middle finger. Then he started flicking them at me. Big cherubic grin. I couldn't believe the audacity. He clearly didn't know I was number three. I did the only reasonable thing. I challenged him to a fight. Milena Rowland tried to warn me; she had seen him lift his bicycle into the air with one hand. He was fat, but he was strong. She knew. He agreed to meet me after school, near his house, or in the field outside, didn't matter to him. He'd meet me anywhere, but he didn't push the issue either. I began to believe Milena Rowland.

Overbaugh lived up near Bacon. When school let out that day, I walked my usual way along the gravel drive, out to the lower part of Henrietta. I was more than relieved when he headed home in the opposite direction, out the paved main entrance to the school. He seemed to think it was funny, both of us looking over one shoulder. A few days later he caught me in a bear hug from behind and picked me up and carried me around for a minute or two, laughing all the while, just to let me know.

Donny had curly, dark hair, dark eyes, and ruddy chipmunk cheeks. He was not like some of the other bigger kids in the class. He was fast. He would have made a great defensive tackle or middle linebacker, though he was over the weight limit for Little Giants football. He never played little league baseball or basketball and dropped out of school before he had the chance to play for the freshman, JV, or varsity football teams. Donny didn't like to practice. He didn't like following anyone else's schedule and wouldn't put up with a coach yelling at him.

After I went away to college and then to graduate school, my father used to tell me that Donny would come down to the church to ask for whatever handouts my father had to give, not an ounce of shame about him, shouting as he came in, *Hello, Mr. Haven!* as if they were old, close friends. He had a wife and kids by then. He was bright and easily could have gone to a good college. Soon after his arrival at Bacon Elementary, Donny was hanging out with Frank and me, and then with other kids from the West End—John Ripepi, Joe Battaglia, Mark DiCaprio, Steven DiBacco. On our provincial scale of things he was a white Moses Malone, banging the boards, shooting and dribbling with both hands. In football no one could tackle him. When he ran the ball, we'd let him get a step past us. Then we'd jump on his back to slow him down while the rest of us clawed at his legs. Also, he could pound a baseball.

Even Pags conceded the issue without having to find out in a fight: Overbaugh was the strongest kid in our sixth-grade class. That didn't mean OB felt the need to challenge Paglietta's tendency to run everything. When our sixth-grade basketball team elected two captains, Pags received the most votes. I was second. Pags decided that meant that he was captain and I was co-captain. My father laughed at that. "If there are two captains then you are both co-captains." Pags didn't see it that way, and that meant none of us did.

Pags only occasionally overstepped his authority, as far as our teachers and principal were concerned, though some of the kids in our class would have voiced a different opinion on that one. Once, the teachers called his parents in over their son's obsession with Benito Mussolini. Pags had begun to draw swastikas on the inside covers of his notebooks. His father put an end to that. Still, his influence over us began to spill into areas other than fights and sports.

One day in sixth grade I noticed a lot of whispering and notes being passed back and forth during the half hour we had in the library. That usually meant a fight after school. I asked Pags what was going on, a fight or something? "Not a fight, Harc, a fuck, *a fuck!*" That was the year we had sex education in science class. Crazy old Mr. Morgan, who once carried a kid by his hair all the way down to the principal's office, grinned from ear to ear as he showed us a film prefaced, "Warning: For Boys Only." We later heard from the girls that they saw the exact same film, the one difference being the subhead, "Warning: For Girls Only."

Mr. Morgan looked like a mild version of Jerry Lewis, complete with the crew cut and 220-volt grin. It was as if the electrical switch that charged his smile was permanently jammed in the *on* position. Mr. Morgan lived in my neighborhood, in one of the old Victorians, a block and a half down Guy Park Avenue. We could count on him each year to buy whatever we were selling in door-to-door church or school fundraisers—Christmas candles, magazine subscriptions, chocolate-covered almonds shaped like footballs. My parents would try to convince my brothers and me to leave him alone during a fundraiser, as he always bought something from each one of us, and probably from any student lucky enough to find Mr. rather than Mrs. Morgan grinning at the door.

More likely Mr. Morgan's grin was fueled by a daily mega overdose of vitamin C. Mr. Morgan talked so often about the panacea of vitamin C that some kids began to leave oranges and empty cardboard cylinders of frozen OJ on his desk when he wasn't looking. He'd laugh and hold the oranges up for the class, and tell us that nature needed a little super charge from human energies—that we would have to eat one hundred oranges to get to the level of vitamin C he was talking about. That's what science was, he'd tell us: observing natural processes, natural energies, and using human intelligence to nudge nature in directions that were beneficial to us. You had to concentrate the stuff, he'd tell us, squeeze one hundred oranges down to the size of a pill.

During sex education Mr. Morgan tried to convey to us the full metaphoric possibilities. "It's like sliding a fat plug into a slick socket, and about as electric! It's more fun than going to the World's Fair!" He pointed out the gerbils in the classroom when they were going at it. When someone asked what would happen if a guy were too big and a girl too small: "It almost always fits, and snug is better!" It was news to me and news, I think, to almost every one of my friends.

Some of the girls were a step ahead of us on that one. One Italian girl in our class had a crush on Richard Podowski, who was a year ahead of us and already in junior high school. She wanted to have sex with him. Pags lived right across the street from Podowski and was trying to arrange it. It was probably just hubris on her part, but she was a good-looking girl and claimed to be all for it. Pags planned to watch. It all fell through when Dowski chickened out.

Pags still ran the show, despite Overbaugh's occasional veto. Sometimes Donny had a moderating influence on Pags, on the rare occasion when Pags would still try to bully us. Though Donny could not always be bothered to step in, sometimes he would simply say "let him go," and Pags would swear and release us, or call one of us a wuss, or say sarcastically to me, *Poopy on you, Harc, poopy on you!* Those were the years when my friends had begun to swear. Still my father's child, I had yet to accept the roadside seat that Amsterdam offered me on some worn interchange between the sacred and the profane.

5

Summer Home

I have always loved my father and grew to love him more the summer I spent alone with him, when I was fourteen years old. I suppose I thought he was a saint until my sophomore year, and then began to view him as most teenagers do their parents, more critically through adolescent eyes. In many ways the summer I spent alone with him marked the beginning of some kind of end. The rest of the family had gone to Martha's Vineyard for the entire sun-soaked stretch of that upstate New York summer. We stayed at home, till August anyway. We had breakfast and dinner together and spent our days apart. We went to church on Sundays, both of us on the altar. By then I had begged my way out of the choir, which was off for the summer anyway. I began to serve as an acolyte.

What I remember of my fourteenth summer is especially one baseball game, my father in the crowd a full head above many of the other spectators. For a while, that was the only baseball game I remembered him attending, though I played for five seasons. Except for the splash of white in his clerical collar, he was dressed entirely in black—his shirt, his shoes, his pants, his raincoat. Every now and then I would hear him shout, "Let's go, Stephen!" When it was my turn to hit, when I was on the on-deck circle, swinging two bats to lighten the thirty-two ounces I would eventually wield at the plate, my father didn't actually come down out of the stands to whisper, low enough for no one else to hear: "Don't worry about it if you strike out." Still, I heard him with my inner ear. He had said as much to me and my younger brother many times before. Even then that seemed like a strange remark. *Tell me to hit a home run, Dad! Tell me to kick some butt!* My father was not strong on killer instinct. He would watch professional football games on television without caring one way or the other who would win.

36

I played baseball for the St. Agnello's Club. The year before, St. Agnello's had won the local little league championship. I was a first baseman on that championship team. The summer I spent with my father, in my last year on St. Agnello's, we lost most of our starters to the high school Rookie League. The coach put me and the diminutive Mike Mancini on the mound. St. Agnello's went 3–11. I pitched the entire game my father attended—seven innings against the best team in the league. We were expected to get crunched. It was one of the coldest days of late spring, after two days of rain. Even though it was early June, it was so damp and cold you could feel the crack of the bat ride up your arms and shatter somewhere in your spine. Both teams had molasses in their veins in the batter's box. With two out in the bottom of the last inning, we were down 2–1. We advanced a runner to third base and then someone whiffed. Though we lost the game, the coach was so happy with the way we played that he took us all to Stewart's Ice Cream.

I was one of the worst pitchers in the league, but my father was convinced that I was a winner on the basis of that one game. He talked about it even in his old age, about a month after he almost died of double pneumonia.

"You were certainly quite a pitcher in your time," my father said, in the living room of his home in Zanesville, Ohio, where he and my mother moved to be near my older brother and me.

"Actually, that's not true, Dad. I was a lousy pitcher. Baseball was never really my game."

"Oh, I don't know, you pitched quite well that one day. A four-hitter, I believe."

"You just think that, Dad, because that was the only game you ever saw."

"I saw quite a few of your games. You must be misremembering. You were quite a pitcher that summer."

I would throw the ball as hard as I could, right over the plate. It had no movement whatsoever. I hadn't learned to kick my leg up and swing my body into the pitch. My pitch was all arm. My friends Bobby Greco and Mark DiCaprio each hit home runs off me that summer. I could practically see them salivate when they came up to swing at the meatballs I hung over the plate.

Once my father mentioned it, I remembered him at the all-star game. Each team chose two players. He didn't remember that I dropped a fly ball in the outfield. He remembered the earlier four-hitter.

"I know there was a lot going on that summer, Dad."

"More than you could imagine. You were just a boy. I had meetings in the evenings, work during the day. There was the yard to take care of, and painting the house, and dinner, and dishes to clean."

On the day we thought he would die, a priest came in from St. Luke's Episcopal Parish, in Granville, Ohio. My father had coded the night before. He was in intensive care. They used the paddles on him. His heart raced up to two hundred beats per minute. The morning the priest came it was still striking steady at 120. We thought he was dying because his heart raced in a similar way the day before and then went into arrhythmia. My older brother and I took Communion with him for what we thought was the last time. We barely made it through the Lord's Prayer. My mother was home resting after her nightlong vigil in my father's hospital room. My sister was driving in from upstate New York. Then my father started talking about his own father, how he had many questions to ask him, and refused to go into detail. He also talked about his boyhood camp counselor, David Dellinger, the former Union Theological Seminary student whose biography had just come out from New York University Press. Then he told me that he never for a moment thought he was going to die the night before:

"I'll tell you what I'm going to do. I'm going to get a hold of my GP and ask him to get me the hell out of here." My father was taller than the hospital bed was long. Though he had only 20 percent lung capacity—permanent damage in his lungs—within a week he was home.

By the end of that week my father had become a Derek Jeter fan. What else was there to do evenings in the hospital? He watched Yankee baseball. My brother Mark and I kidded him: "You're a Buckeye now. Forget the Yankees!" Then we asked him how, after a lifetime of not caring about professional baseball, a little time in the hospital had turned him into a Derek Jeter fan.

"I am not actually a Derek Jeter fan," he said. "He simply has re- markable baseball skills, and I admire that in him."

Even on the verge of his death, my father had a formal bearing, despite his occasional off-color humor. He kept thanking the nurses. He reminded me of his mother, my grandmother, after medics picked her up from a nursing home and took her on a final drive to the hospital. My grand- mother was conscious enough in the emergency room to insist that we be sure to thank the ambulance driver.

"I am sorry you are going through this now," my older brother said in my father's living room. "You have had a wonderful life. I am sorry you are in this tough spot now."

"It is what it is," my father said. He still had ten months to live.

All the years I lived at home with him, hardly anyone other than my father's immediate boyhood family called him Rob or Robbie. It seemed that no one called him Robert or plain old Bob. It was as if people didn't know how to address him—as if he had no name other than one that would identify him by his vocation. He was dark-haired, six foot three, 205 pounds, thin and strong. He had powerful forearms. On more than one occasion I have been in the presence of women who thought my father was as handsome a man as they had ever known. He decidedly did not play basketball or football but had a little baseball in him. He was a physical man, though not necessarily in an athletic sort of way. Though he was gentle with children, you could see the raw physical side of him when he cut kindling for the fire we kept burning all winter long, or when he shoveled snow, or ran the snow blower while the rest of us shoveled, or while in summer he mowed.

His friends in college called him Marsh. For reasons I didn't entirely understand until I was more than forty years old, my mother never called him anything other than Rev. He was *Reverend* to almost everyone outside the church and *Father Haven* to almost everyone in it. Only his closest church friends called him Father Bob, and that usually outside regular church hours, in the quiet, intimate setting of their homes or ours. For years it seemed strange to me that no one seemed to call him by his given name, but when the octogenarian in him leaned toward some new absence, it seemed less strange, as if he lived above or beyond and not only *through* his name, this father who has stayed with me everywhere I have ever been.

I do not particularly believe in ghosts or in visitations. I don't like to talk about the unseen world because it is beyond human comprehension, or anyway beyond the ability of language to render precisely the weight of its insistent presence. I know very well that nothing has meaning until we can name it—until language brings to it some degree of measure. I know too that whatever language names cannot be summed up by the words we assign to the *you* of it, or to the *me, myself, and I,* or to the simplest *it* of it. Through the act of naming, as Theodore Roethke has it, we dare to spread our wings against the vast immeasurable emptiness of things.

In my dream my grandfather was sitting in my father's favorite chair, in our living room, before the fire. I make no claims for that moment except that I woke up suddenly from it and have remembered it clearly for nearly thirty years. My grandfather had been dead for seven years. I was in college. In the other armchair of the living room, there was another grandfather, and though he had no body, no visible shape at all, I knew the energy there was my mother's father, who died before I was born. I sidled up to the familiar bodily presence of my Grandfather Haven. He was tall and lanky like my father, spread out in the armchair, leaning toward my side. Unlike my father, he regarded me with a half smirk and a glint in his eye, as if everything were almost always half a joke. I said the most inane thing—"I play the cello"—though that was hardly true, only two years into my attempt to take the instrument seriously after many years of fooling around. My grandfather simply looked at me and said nothing, though it was a warm silence. I was in awe of that other presence and afraid of it, too, pulsing from across the room.

In a similar sort of way my father has stayed with me through every single moment, every location and relocation of my life. During my childhood years, in Lent we had Wednesday potluck dinners—the one evening church activity my mother would attend. On Tuesdays and Thursdays we had boys' choir rehearsals. We had church basketball practice one winter evening per week, and on Friday or Saturday night we played a game. As long as I was still singing in the church choir—through to the end of the eighth grade—I was with my father during Lent at some sort of church event six days a week. Maybe that is why it seems as though he is always with me now, because he was with me so often then. If my brothers and I were singing in the choir room, he was reading in the light of his office at the other end of the parish hall. Before and after basketball, he'd talk with the coach and with the older boys. Even as a child, I knew that my father's parishioners had nothing but the deepest respect for him.

My father was an early riser. He was the first thing I heard every morning. He was up at 6 A.M., weekdays and weekends, always glad to start the day. I think it was something that began in the navy, just at the close of World War II, and then became second nature to him. Mornings, I would hear him shaving with an electric razor. Then he would take a bath, all six foot three of him stretched out in our porcelain, lion-clawed tub. We had no shower until I was in the eleventh grade. If we had to pee early in the morning, we'd walk right in on him, the boys anyway.

Then it was eggs and bacon in the kitchen, my mother still sleeping. Later, as he got older, it was simply toast and coffee, though he would still cook breakfast for all the kids who got up early on Saturdays, basting the eggs in bacon fat in a cast iron frying pan, to create the over-easy effect without having to flip anything. My father couldn't cook much of anything other than eggs and a few dishes he relied upon as a standard repertoire when my mother was gone. Nothing fancier than Shake 'N Bake chicken or boiled hot dogs.

Sometimes, early on a Saturday morning, he'd take one of us to Tulio's Diner for an early breakfast. "What'll it be, Reverend?" the short order cook would sling out. My father did not like to be called Reverend.

"Ya got the boy with you today?"

"Sure do."

Then it was anything off the menu. I usually went for French toast and a couple of links.

Tulio's was a classic, silver-trailer-type diner, where the local churches would send homeless men for a hot meal. My father had coupons to hand out to anyone who would come by the church asking for money. He would never give out cash as he knew the odds were that it wouldn't be spent on food. Sometimes those men would be thankful, and sometimes they would get angry when my father would give them only meal tickets and no money. Sometimes the homeless would come by when my parents were not around. That was always a frightening moment for my brothers, my sister, and me. Some of them would bang their fists on the thick wooden door of the church. We didn't know where my father kept those meal coupons. He would tell us not to open the door when he was not in, but sometimes we did anyway. On the few evenings when I encountered those men alone, they stood in the gaunt porch light of the church, sick with the thought that the minister was not able to help them. Once, when I was nearly in high school, one man refused to take no for an answer, until I slammed the door. Some part of my early childhood was haunted by those grown men, desperate enough for food that they would beg it from a boy.

Monday evening church basketball began when I was in the third grade. I loved the smell of the leather basketballs, the low thud of them off the wooden floorboards, and the high-pitched staccato of sneakers as the older boys cut and drilled. Third graders played right along with the high school kids, or shot baskets while the older kids ran plays at the other end of the court, or simply sat on the bench and watched. There weren't enough Protestant children in the town to organize the league by age. That made for some fairly ragtag teams. Any Protestant church team with a group of five high school players would steam roll other churches in the league. The losing coaches would send up the white flag and then both teams would put the little kids into the game. Though my father loved to see St. Ann's win, he came to the games mainly because those evenings were part of the church community—the older boys rooting for the elementary school kids as they scored their first baskets, the younger boys idolizing basketball gods who would soon graduate from high school and head off to college or jobs.

Almost every year some of the older players in our church would make the Amsterdam High varsity basketball team, which made them ineligible for church ball. My father thought their loyalties should be with the parish. I took those comments to heart. That meant I played with my church team until I graduated and never tried out for varsity. Maybe I was trying to keep from disappointing my father. For years, when I continued to play ball in my twenties and thirties, I regretted missing the formal drills of a high school basketball program. "I could have been a contender, I could have been somebody," Marlon Brando says in *On the Waterfront*—lines that must resonate, in all likelihood, in almost every human life. I hear them in the context of the old armory gym. I might have sat the bench, but I was good enough to have played high school ball.

My father would come regularly to my church basketball games and every fall Sunday afternoon to my Little Giants football games, but not more than once or twice to baseball, at least in my memory of things. I never really gave it too much thought when I was a boy. I rode my bicycle to the high school and to the Bacon Elementary School diamonds. The presence of fathers at those games seemed more the exception than the rule. I never once remember seeing Woody's father standing along the first or third base lines, or sitting on the chipped green paint of the wooden stands, or hovering over the umpire's shoulder, where, if he were ever there, we might have seen him through the chained links of the backstop, as if in some cubist portrait of a man.

I never once saw Frank Johnson's stepfather at a Little Giants game and don't remember his mother there either. I know with certainty that my mother never attended a single sporting event that I ever played. I only think of this now that I am a father, with children active in sports. I know there were vestry meetings. I know my father attended all sorts of other meetings for community organizations outside the church. He helped establish a local legal aid society and organized a day-care center for indigent women. But how many evening meetings could there have been?

Maybe my father came to my Little Giants games because I couldn't very well have found my own way there by bicycle, what with shoulder pads and cleats and a helmet that would have dangled off one handlebar. Maybe those Sunday afternoons were the end of his work week—he always had Mondays off—when he was ready to spend a little time outside the church with the kids. Maybe there was something about the evening hour that my father disliked—my baseball games taking place near or after 5 P.M. Maybe in summer, when there were no choir rehearsals until school started again, my father could actually stay home four or five nights per week, and so relaxed into the long-shadowed, soft light of June and the lull of July, before packing the family up and heading down to the ocean in August.

Or maybe it was the cocktail hour that sapped the energy of the evening and sent my mother and father to the haven of their own living room, where the light of summer slowly waned and they fell asleep before the television by 10 P.M., as I so often do now, what with rising at dawn, the chaos of my own kids, a couple of microbrewed beers, dinner and dishes and all.

My father had a natural dignity about him that an argument with my mother or a few drinks gone sour sometimes undid in him. Scotch on the rocks, a Manhattan or two, an extra dry martini or a few, became a ritual at 5 P.M. for my parents and my grandparents. A hard drink with the neighbors was the secret sign of brotherhood, and sisterhood, too, for those generations. Maybe my father needed to be a regular guy at the end of the day, and a couple of drinks with family or friends got him there, or almost there. It was mainly then that my father vented—not always, not every night, only on occasion—whatever sarcasm he had in him.

"Stephen, would you mind moving your hair to the other side of the room?" my father asked me in high school one summer, one of the more memorable moments in our continual banter over the barbershop.

"Would you mind passing the cancer?" my father would say after dinner when he wanted to sweeten his coffee with saccharine instead of sugar.

My parents were having marriage problems during the summer I spent at home alone with my father. Some years before, they bought a cottage in Oak Bluffs, on Martha's Vineyard, for four thousand dollars. They borrowed the money—about half of my father's salary—from my Grandmother Harcourt. She didn't ask them to pay against the principal—they only made interest payments—though I am sure, in many other ways, in principle they paid. In order to finance the loan, my parents thought they would rent the cottage out to tenants for all but a month of each summer. That plan fell by the wayside during the summer of my fourteenth year.

Throughout my entire childhood, I never once threw a football with my father, never once shot baskets with him either. We painted the house together, chopped wood, and dug our way out of each upstate New York winter storm. We mowed and raked the lawn. Though we later played tennis and raquetball when I was in college, my father moved in different circles than I did in my childhood daily routine of sports with neighborhood friends. Still, that summer, in our backyard, in my only memory of playing ball with my father, he would come out after dinner to sizzle grounders to Donny Overbaugh and me. Overbaugh wasn't afraid to square up in front of those shots. I backed away.

Our Martha's Vineyard summer home was a gingerbread cottage, built within a few feet of our next-door neighbor. The previous owner's wooden sign *Compensation* still hung in our minds from the eaves of the front porch. When my parents bought the place, the first thing they did was to take *Compensation* down, *as if there were anything else in our lives that required compensation!* We owned the cottage, but the land on which it was built was a song that belonged to the Methodist Campground. That arrangement allowed the Methodist Campground Association the option of forcing any of the wilder families out. No one I knew was ever forced out. More than one campground cocktail party ended up on the lawn of the Methodist Tabernacle, where every Wednesday evening we would take part in a community sing. We sang songs everyone knew, as there were no hymnals. "Take Me Out to the Ball Game," "Swing Low, Sweet Chariot."

My mother retreated to the Vineyard the summer of my fourteenth year. She took my two brothers and my sister with her. I stayed with my father, in part to play little league ball. I remember that marital discord mainly in flashes—a few downright zingers and a few intense family talks about two households, both of them equally ours, one in Amsterdam, one in Saratoga Springs, where my mother, having completed a Masters degree, had begun to work as a lecturer in sociology at Skidmore College. Those flashes of discord grew larger in amplitude and shorter in range as my parents aged.

One night, prior to her departure for the Vineyard, my mother sat the whole family down in our living room to ask us an important question. My father didn't say a word, though he looked worried. There was no mention of a divorce or a separation. Where would we prefer to live? The new arrangement was simply going to be a matter of convenience, to cut down on my mother's half-hour commute. I wondered if the new house in Saratoga

Springs would include a horse. My mother assured me that a horse was a possibility.

Why was I home with my father that summer? Why was I the child to keep my father company? The party was on Martha's Vineyard, at the beach. My parents did not require me to stay in Amsterdam for the stretch of that season. I chose to stay at home. Baseball was not the only compelling reason.

My father once told me over drinks, during a vacation on Cape Cod after we had sold our Martha's Vineyard cottage, that suffering was the meaning of life. He said this straight out without inviting me or anyone to discuss the point. We were sitting on a deck in the backyard of a summer home we had rented for a few weeks, just outside of Wellfleet. I was twenty-five years old. I have no idea what gave rise to that remark. I told him that any number of his parishioners would dispute that point with him. I said, what about the birth of a baby? There is suffering in that but joy too. He said suffering comes around in the end. I didn't push the issue, as I knew the optimist in my father was a morning person—that evening would sometimes swallow him in the smoke of his own Tipparillos. I knew that dawn would bring him round again.

In a light Luminist painters would have loved, shimmering off water and sand, as if land and sea were blurred in the pulse of one overwhelming sheen, my father frightened me. Though it makes more sense to me now, I remember inwardly recoiling from the notion that suffering was in some way the heart of human experience. I remember thinking that at least some part of a meaningful life involved dancing with a woman you had just that evening met until the bar closed down.

It was mainly in the evening, too, that my father would lay into Nixon with the true passion of a convert. It wouldn't matter to my father if everyone in the room was a dyed-in-the-wool Republican. I remember one cocktail hour in particular when my grandfather and my father argued over Vietnam. *"Damn it, Robbie! Damn it!"* my grandfather yelled. When I reminded my father of that moment in the year before he died, he said, "There were so many more important things we could have talked about." When I chimed in that my grandfather said, *"God* damn it, Robbie!" my father was quick to correct me: "He never said *'God.'* He would never have said *'God* damn.' "

It must have been tough being a priest 24–7. One does not retire from that station at the end of a working life, and one does not leave it behind at the end of the work day. The dying won't wait for a priest to finish a drink, or a dinner, or a vacation, or a good night's sleep. Maybe it is hard to imagine the dark moments that occur in the life of a minister. My father's church had 150 families. In the heyday of St. Ann's, on Christmas and Easter, the church would bring more than 250 people into the midnight or 10 A.M. service. There were many more parishioners who never came. How many funerals per year does a priest perform in a church that size? Part of a priest's job was to look death straight in the eye, in the most tangible way, in the weekly company of a corpse, not to mention the grieving families, and come back celebrating the sure promise of living. One of our parishioners, a farmer, backed out of his driveway and ran over his own three-year-old son. What could my father say? The phone would ring in our home at any time of night. We would feel the adrenalin jolt and my father would rush off.

Maybe my father meant that suffering *with dignity* was the basis for real meaning in life, or suffering within a belief in meaning beyond the immediate experience of pain. Or maybe he meant that as physical beings, suffering is programmed into us, and therefore any belief in God must take place within that context.

Maybe my father needed a couple of drinks at the end of the work day to become a regular guy again, something other than a symbol of his office. Whenever I was out in town with my father, it was always, "Hiya, Reverend. How are ya, Father," the spotlight right on him, even if he didn't wear his collar.

As if a name could contain anyone, as if my father might be tallied by three words only, the engraver of the Albany Cemetery has chiseled *Robert Marshall Haven* into stone. *"One need not be a Chamber to be Haunted,"* as Dickinson says. *"One need not be a House . . . ."*

Every Sunday, as a boy in Amsterdam, I would listen to my father's sermons. I would weigh his words, as I knew he would ask me for my thoughts when we came home from church. Now I don't remember much of anything he said from the pulpit. What I remember is a presence. I don't know if that presence was an embodiment of something my father had actually attained, or if it was something he aimed at, missed, and continued always through the deepest part of his nature to aim at nevertheless. Though my father was sometimes tough to talk to in the evening, he also knew something about deep listening. "We are not good listeners," he once wrote in a parish newsletter:

> In conversation, when someone talks to us, we are often so filled with our own thoughts that we only half listen if we listen at all. It is because our own thoughts are more interesting to us. Sometimes we break in upon the person talking to us and interrupt him, not even extending to him the courtesy of hearing him out. Sometimes we hear the person out and then speak of a similar experience from our own lives, thereby making the case of the person talking to us only an illustration of our own . . . .
>
> There is the Grace of God in selfless listening. It is true that one of the steps on the climb to holiness is to learn to listen. Listening is an epiphany. In listening we find Christ who said, "he who has ears to hear, let him hear." Let us pray, then, that God will grant us ears.

My father knew something about seeing the human being in front of him instead of the vocation, the ideology, gender, or skin. As much as he often failed what he knew, I saw him live by it every day, too. Maybe that helped him serve successfully in a series of northern, southern and midwestern churches at a time when the Episcopal Church was deeply divided by American culture wars. Maybe it helped that my father was a navy man and that he was also a writer and welcomed the church as the primary vehicle in his life for a close, visceral contact with people, in the widest possible range of human experience. Maybe it helped him, too, that he valued his own solitude and valued as fully the rhythms of his family. It was enough for him, early in the quiet of the morning, his children around him, his wife still sleeping, an office that brushed the entire compass of a life, and the spirit warmed like air into breath in the house of the new day.

It is a strange and beautiful thing to have in one's father the only priest one will ever fully embrace. I would not necessarily recommend it to anyone, though it has been one of the more powerful influences in my life. One should not speak too often or openly about the still center my father encouraged in others and found so often in himself. As any Old Testament scholar would know, whatever name it has been given, whatever liturgies have been assigned to it, no human utterance is equal to the task of summing it. It is only right, then, that one should hush oneself in the presence of its human name. What moved in my father leaned its slow way toward me. It was worth any number of missed baseball games.

6

Tryon

Ninth grade was a transitional year for me. I stopped playing football after summer practices, just before the start of the freshman season. The following spring, on the roof of the McNulty Elementary School, I smoked my first joint and soon stopped hanging out in the West End with my Italian friends. That was the beginning of some real change. But first there were the slow years of Theodore Roosevelt Junior High School. During those middle school years, in warm weather, after school and on weekends, my friends in the West End practically lived with me on John Ripepi's basketball court, a rectangular black top that did not need to serve double duty as a driveway.

Rat, as we called him, lived on Tryon Street, one and a half blocks from my home. He was a tall, sweet, skinny kid, whose father ran a numbers racket out of Tom's Lunch, a snack bar a couple of miles from the neighborhood. Rat Ripepi was the only boy in the neighborhood to have a court with a pole sunk in concrete, though the entire basket shook every time we banked a shot in. Rat would actually say "youse" instead of "you," as in "youse guys" and "where are all of youse going," as if in some bad parody of an Italian accent. When Rat's sister stunk up the bathroom, Rat would announce it loud enough for all of us to hear: "Oh my God, Jennifer, what'd something die in there?!" Jennifer would laugh and blush, "Shut up, Johnny! Whoose talkin'?! Look whoose talkin, Johnny! You little shit-ass, you!" On the court, shit was the x-factor, the rabbit's foot, the elemental mythic agent of fate and good luck. If someone hit an improbable, game-winning shot, one of us would yell out, "Check his shoes! That shot's got shit all over it." That's how Pags's "poopy on you" routine got started. Until I was in the ninth grade, I refused to say anything stronger than *darn*.

My father almost fell out of his chair the night Tom Ripepi appeared handcuffed on the evening news, charged with racketeering. But Tom Ripepi's son was a straight arrow—never got involved with drugs, hardly drank as a teenager, and eventually married his high school sweetheart, Cookie Medwin. Until the end of ninth grade, Rat's court was our main hangout, where my friends and I spent almost every spring, summer, and autumn day. Rat actually liked anchovies on his pizza, the true mark, as far as we were concerned, of a genuine Italian. We moved right in to Rat's backyard and staked out our claim to his front porch, playing APBA baseball—a dice game with a card for each professional player, statistically based on the previous Major League Baseball season. The river was half a block away. We could smell it from where we played, when the air hung hot and heavy above the water.

Sometimes Mark DiCaprio would come down. He lived four or five blocks further west on Division Street. Sometimes the older kids would also play with and against us—Billy Johnson and his friends, Danny Agresta, Pat Emerick, Steven DiBacco's older brother John. Otherwise it was Overbaugh and me, Frank, Steven DiBacco, and Rat's best friend Joe Battag. Occasionally kids in the grade behind us would play, like Mike Leonetti, who lived right down the street from Frank, or Tony DiBacco, Steven's younger brother.

In winter, Danny Agresta and his brother Ham ran a blackjack table in the basement of their house. We played a quarter a hand, one card up for the dealer, everyone else two cards down. Blackjack and five cards and under paid double. You could go down for double with a ten or an eleven—one hit only, down and dirty. I don't know if those blackjack games were on the up and up, as the dealers always seemed to win. Usually only Overbaugh and the Agrestas and the DiBaccos had enough money to take the deal and cover the bets of the seven or eight of us around the table. The Agrestas had these incredibly big, juicy oranges their parents brought back each year from Florida. Sometimes they would break them out, one for each of us. They cost their parents a quarter apiece.

Summers, on Saturday afternoons, when the West End factories closed at noon, we'd play fast-pitch rubber ball in one of the mill yards. The mill yard was so narrow that you couldn't pull the ball or hit to what would normally be right field. A shot to what would be the left field upper deck would break a window. Frank would always cup a hand to his ear then raise a fist if he heard glass. There were already so many broken windows that no one ever seemed to notice or care. The windows were painted green. They opened by pulling a chain attached to the upper end of a metal frame. The tops of the windows swung in, the bottoms out. Home plate was beneath a big green overhead walkway that rose at a forty-five-degree angle, connecting one factory building to another. A ground-rule double was a straight shot that bounced off the chain fence on the other side of Gardner Street. A home run cleared the fence.

Otherwise, it was football, through to the fall of my ninth- grade year. It was mainly through Frank and Billy's influence that I first began to play football at the beginning of fourth grade. There was never any question in the Johnson family that their boys would play ball. No one in my family ever had. The summer before fourth grade, Frank and I were already playing tackle with Billy and the older kids. When August neared, clutching jars of urine we lined up in the sun outside Doctor Pipito's office, a small yellow house on Guy Park Avenue, close to downtown. Across the street, in an old gas station, they handed out rib and shoulder pads, helmets, and cleats. Dr. Pipito, a tall athletic-looking man of about sixty, with thick, snow-white hair, poked us between testicle and thigh, all the while smoking a cigar. Mr. Miller—president of the Little Giants Football League, brother of my father's church organist, and coach of the Purple team—weighed us in. He had an incredibly large head, dark hair, and black pinhole eyes.

On cold November days Mr. Miller would stand along the sidelines shouting out plays, his fingers tucked inside his belt, as the groin—as he told his boys—was the warmest spot in the body. On cold days, the Purple team always had their hands halfway down their pants. Billy Johnson was already on Purple, so we knew that Frank would be. The league kept brothers together. The weight limit was 140. No one over 115 pounds could run the ball. Mr. Miller tended to look the other way when the Purple kids weighed in. Some of his kids pushed the scales close to 160. He always seemed to snag for his team the biggest of the new recruits. Purple usually won the championship each year. That meant Frank was headed for a winner. I took the luck of the draw and my luck was Green.

I don't remember the name of the Green team's coach but he was dating Miss Lockhart, the music teacher who rented the third-floor apartment above our house. That meant we could see the coach from our kitchen, using our back porch to access Miss Lockhart's stairs. The coach was a gym teacher in one of the elementary schools. Maybe he resented that Miss Lockhart had a built-in chaperone. He always seemed to have a chip on his shoulder when he'd run into me in my backyard, or when I caught his eye through the kitchen screen door. Maybe the fact that I knew his girlfriend, and that he knew my father was a minister, didn't improve my rating on his toughness register. The year of my first Little Giants season, it was 1966. I was nine. The Summer of Love hadn't happened yet and anyway never quite came to Amsterdam, New York. As liberal as my father was in opposing war, he believed with his whole being in the institution of marriage: no twenty-four- hour visitation for any single man or woman who rented either of our apartments, the one on the third floor of our house, the other over the garage. The coach didn't push the limits. Maybe Miss Lockhart didn't allow it. In any case, I didn't score any points for running into him, off the field, with beautiful blonde Miss Lockhart on his arm as he mounted her stairs.

Like high school football in many other mill towns, the Wilbur H. Lynch High football program was a regional powerhouse, probably because the city of Amsterdam had boys in pads and helmets from the age of nine on. The little league coaches were serious. We had daily, three-hour practices for the last two weeks of summer. We dogged it on laps around the high school's four baseball diamonds, did wind sprints and "Green Bays"—running in place, our knees high, touching our outstretched palms. We'd hit the ground every time the coach whistled us down, then pop back up again. Pushups, jumping jacks, bridges to strengthen our backs and necks. Then pads: We dug in and drove the blocking sleds. Those first few weeks my entire body was sore, from my feet to the tip of my nose. Once school began, we practiced twice weekly, from 5 P.M. until it got dark. In the fourth grade, even though I was a little skinny at eighty pounds, I had good bones. Miss Lockhart's boyfriend put me on the line. I didn't mind getting hit. I actually grew to love the contact.

I can't remember exactly when it was, in the second season or at the beginning of the third, that the coach of the Green team scheduled one of our twice-weekly practices on a night that conflicted with my choir rehearsal. The coach was incredulous. He practically made me stand up on a bench and sing. There was no way he would excuse my missing practice one day per week. I would sit the bench. What was I, some kind of sissy? He started calling me "The Mighty Fortress," for "A Mighty Fortress Is Our God." When I missed a tackle, when I hit a runner high rather than down at his knees, he would say, "That doesn't look much like a fortress to me!" My father took care of this situation by having me transferred to another team. Thank God for the Maroon Wildcats and the tempered Mr. Sculcos of the world!

Mr. Sculco, the Maroon coach, was an older, more mature man, tough on his team but without ever demeaning anyone. He lived a couple of doors down from Frank Johnson on Division Street. Mr. Sculco started me at offensive guard and defensive tackle. By then I weighed over one hundred pounds. It helped that our best running back, Glen Taylor—one of the few black kids in the city—once sang in my church choir. Glen would eventually play cornerback on our high school varsity, and Salvatore Battaglia, who took snaps for the Maroon Wildcats, would quarterback that team. My last year in the Little Giants, when I was in the eighth grade, the Maroon Wildcats went a respectable 8–2, finishing second only to Purple. Still, at the end of each of those seasons, Frank had bragging rights and didn't fail to use them.

A knee operation at the beginning of my freshman year ended my brief football career. By trade I was a lineman, but puberty hadn't fully kicked in for me. It may have been a good thing the knee operation clipped short my freshman season. The largest guys on the line were pushing 175 pounds. More than likely it was patella instability that caused my knees to ache after every football practice, the full effects of which I wouldn't feel for another twenty-eight basketball years. There was a suspicious spot on the X-ray. The doctors thought I had a tumor or a broken bone. They opened me up about five inches on the inside of my left knee and found nothing. The scar was an inch-wide centipede. The nerves grew back in patches, numb spots splotched in with areas of full and partial feeling.

By the time I healed it was late autumn. It was back to Rat Ripepi's yard. We'd play basketball until dusk and then go home to dinner. Donny O would never want the game to end. He never wanted to walk the mile back to his house at dinnertime. Though his stepfather ran a gift shop on the corner of West Main and Gardner Street, right in our neighborhood, he rarely gave his stepson a ride home. Once, trying to put off the onset of the dinner hour, Overbaugh wrapped Steven DiBacco in his arms and refused to let him go to his mother's table until he tapped the ruby red slippers of his Converse sneakers together, three times at the heel, closed his eyes, and said, "There's no place like home, there's no place like home." DiBacco held out for ten or fifteen minutes before he gave in. In the midst of our crazed laughter, he finally played Dorothy to Donny's Glinda.

That was the fall OB would often come home with me and wait in my room while I had dinner with my family. He came home with me so often that my parents stopped inviting him to the table. My mother would send him up a plate of food and wonder why he didn't go to his own home. After dinner we played Skittlebowl or cards until my parents would ask Donny to leave so that I could begin work on geometry or on papers I was writing for honors English.

That was the year too that there were fights in the junior high school that scared the manna out of me. One was between Chris Coleman and Mark Majewski. Pags, as always, was in the middle of things. I thought Pags was Chris's friend, from all the honors classes he and Chris and I shared together, but when the fight began Pags started yelling, "Kick his ass, Majewski, kick his ass!"

Chris was a farm boy, with big arms from bailing hay. There were some forty or fifty kids crowded around them in a vacant lot, most of them shouting. Chris caught Majewski with a shot that broke his nose—blood everywhere, all over Majewski's shirt.

"Majewsk, what happened? Jewski! There's blood on your shirt!" Pags laughed, his way of consoling Majewski after the fight broke up. They were kids in men's bodies and I still hadn't grown.

"One lucky shot," Majewski said. "One lucky shot."

As Wilbur H. Lynch High School was too small a building to handle all four high school grades, Roosevelt Junior High continued through to the end of my freshman year. The school brought me into close contact with kids from all the other neighborhoods in town, including Puerto Ricans from the East End. Puerto Rican families would come up to Amsterdam from New York City to take jobs in the mills. We all thought they were tougher than the local kids, and they knew it and played off that reputation. There were no knives, or chains, or weapons of any kind in the school—that only changed after crack arrived in the 1980s. But some of the Puerto Rican kids wouldn't hesitate to kick you in the balls and knee you in the face on your way down. I remember my ninth grade art teacher, Mr. Bolton, discussing with Pags, right in the middle of class, the odds of Ervin Garcia winning a fight against Tim Szewski. Szewski was an athlete who later turned out to be the best wide receiver and punt returner on the varsity football team. Bolton's money was on Garcia because he thought Szewski didn't have the chutzpah to kick Garcia in the gonads. At any rate, he would have to think twice about it. By then Garcia would have him.

For a couple of weeks in ninth grade, Garcia chose to toy with me in the locker room after school. Garcia would grab my lock and refuse to give it back. Or he'd ask me for a quarter and would haunt my locker every day when I refused to give him any change. It was child's play but seemed at that sensitive age like midnight at all cardinal points, and maelstrom in the sky. I don't remember exactly how I squirmed out of that one, but it might have gone like this:

"Give me a quarter. Let's go," he would say. "Hurry up. I'd hate to have to kick your ass."

"Give me a break. You don't need a quarter."

"A fucking quarter, man! I said a quarter. I am going to have to kick your ass."

"What are you talking about? A quarter moon? A quarter pound of butter? A quarter loaf of bread?"

"Your ass, man! A quarter or your ass!"

"I am *not* going to give you any money, and you are *not* going to kick my ass!"

Then he would give me a shove and I would shrug my shoulders and walk away. I dreaded pulling my books out of the locker room every morning and putting them away at the end of the day. There was absolutely no teacher supervision, maybe because they were half afraid of the kids. I never ended up fighting Garcia and I never gave him any money. I expected Overbaugh to step in, but he found it funny. Overbaugh outweighed Garcia by fifty pounds. Maybe Garcia knew that OB and I were friends and for that reason never followed me out the school door.

That was a transitional year, too, in many other ways. I didn't as much discover girls as Donny Overbaugh discovered one for me. Though Judy Tambasco was, in theory anyway, my girlfriend since elementary days, I hardly ever spoke to her. An actual girlfriend, one I could hold by the hand, came into my life through the payphone across from Spagnolia's Grill, kitty corner to the Division Street Fire House. One night, walking from his house to the West End, Donny heard it ring. A girl named Maria Luisa was in the habit of writing down payphone numbers and calling them with her friends when she was bored, just to see who answered. She gave her number to OB. *Maria Luisa Sulerno,* one of the more musical names I have ever known. Everyone except Maria Luisa's sisters and parents called her Mary Luisa. I usually called her Mary. I owe this one to Donny: It took me nearly two years to get there, but that phone call eventually got me laid.

After Donny answered that mysterious ring, we would dial Mary's number most evenings. We would call her on the phone in my room. Mary lived all the way down in the East End, on the last street of a Puerto Rican neighborhood. The Italians started moving out from the East End a long time ago, when Puerto Rican families started moving in, but Mary's family hung on to their house, and to the one they owned right next door, where Mary would eventually live with her husband, Jimmy Fassio. The Sulerno homes were practically built into and under a factory that loomed over the end of their street.

Mary must have met Donny once or twice because she let me know, one night on the phone, that he was too big for her. We talked for six months, almost every night, before we ever met. Mary attended St. Mary's Catholic School, the one alternative in town to the Theodore Roosevelt Junior High School. That was why I never met her before. Eventually, with her sister Cara and my brother Mark, we met at the Tryon Theater to see a James Bond movie—the one where the bad guys go airborne off a ski jump and land in the blades of a truck-sized snowblower. When red snow arcs from the super-sized chute, Roger Moore cracks, "They sure had a lot of guts." We were too nervous to laugh.

Mary's hair was so straight she might have ironed it, deep black all the compact way down to her butt. She sat so that it hung to one side of her head, a curtain between us. For the entire length of the movie she smiled, more to herself than to me. She was one of the loudest people I ever spoke with on the phone. She would hold three conversations at once, in Italian and English, two with her sisters and one with me. That night at the movies, it was all I could do to say hello. After the long silence of the show, we walked our separate ways home. As soon as we got back to our parents' houses, we talked about nothing I can remember for another hour on the phone.

7

Saratoga Springs

One of the more remarkable things about my mother is that she married a dying man. She must have loved him very deeply to have married him when all the specialists he consulted gave him no more than five years to live. She was very young when she made this decision and somewhat less young when she decided to have four children by him. My Grandfather Harcourt liked very much the man my mother chose to marry but thought his daughter was making a rash decision, as there was no financial plan in the likely event that the doctors would turn out to be right. Sometimes the line between courage and foolishness is so fine that the former blends with the latter and you can't tell one from the other, or so Faulkner tells us in *Go Down, Moses.* Maybe that is what my Grandfather Harcourt said to my mother when she was stubborn enough to believe that she had found her lifelong companion, despite the specialists' prognosis.

There was no cure for Hodgkin's disease in the spring of 1951. My father received the bad news just prior to taking his senior exams at Amherst College. He was a member of a war-veteran class: twenty-five years old. For a moment he wondered whether it was worth bothering with the exams, then took them anyway. Over the next five years he went through a series of operations to carve out tumors from his armpits. During this time, he worked one year as a banker in New York, then enrolled as a student first at the Union Theological Seminary and then at the Episcopal Theological Seminary in Cambridge, Massachusetts. He was given mass doses of radiation, the burns from which were plainly visible when he took off his shirt—mysterious red continents to my brothers and me. He also had internal scars in his chest cavity, which eventually killed him at the age of eighty-one. The scar tissue prevented an open-heart surgery from draining properly. Fluid calcified on both lungs.

As a boy I remember driving with my father from Amsterdam to Syracuse, New York, for his annual check-up with a Hodgkin's disease specialist. My father was the miracle man. To the utter amazement of his doctors, after five years of operations he went into remission and never came out again. He told me that after the initial shock was over, he never again thought he was going to die.

The early diagnosis did not daunt my mother. As a teenager, she spent two years studying music at Smith College and then dropped out after her sophomore year. She moved to New York City where she hoped to continue voice lessons and make her way eventually to Italy. One evening she ran into my father in the Village. It didn't matter to her that he was being treated for cancer. She had met him previously at Amherst. They were five years apart. Goodbye, Italy. Hello, Cambridge. Hello, upstate New York.

My sister was born in Boston, in 1954, my older brother a year later in Binghamton, New York, where my father spent two years as curate to the Reverend W. Paul Thompson at Trinity Church. The story my family tells is that my father turned down a more lucrative position in a Flint, Michigan, Episcopal parish because he had already promised Paul Thompson that he would come to Binghamton and didn't want to break his word. Then in 1956 my father became the priest-in-charge of the newly formed Episcopal mission in Camillus, New York, a few miles from Syracuse. He was appointed rector of St. Luke's Episcopal Church a few years later when the parish was able to support itself. My younger brother Tom and I were both born in Syracuse, in 1957 and 1960. We moved to Amsterdam, New York, in 1961.

According to family legend, my mother cried the day my family arrived in Amsterdam, in an old Ford station wagon, to occupy the St. Ann's rectory on Locust Avenue. She was twenty-nine years old. We moved to be near my grandparents, all three of whom were living in Albany, New York. We moved to be near the Adirondack State Park, thirty miles north of Amsterdam. We moved because the rectory in Amsterdam was larger than the ranch house we occupied in Camillus, where three of the four children in my family slept on beds in the basement. We moved because the seven thousand dollars offered by St. Ann's represented a significant raise for my father.

As an Episcopal priest in the Albany diocese, my father never commanded much of a salary. Each month he would balance the checkbook right down to the penny but never seemed to worry much about finding new ways to feed the coffers. When my mother could stand no more, she insisted that we move out of the rectory and buy our own home. That brought us to our old Victorian, at 253 Guy Park Avenue, when I was eight years old. A few years later, my mother wore my father down sufficiently to buy the gingerbread cottage on Martha's Vineyard. When my parents moved out of Amsterdam they made $100,000 on my boyhood home, and later cleared $40,000 on the gingerbread. Though my mother couldn't be bothered to balance a checkbook, with real estate she had the golden touch. On two later homes she made another $145,000.

It is one thing to marry a dying man when you are twenty-two years old—to live in the immediate moment of love, and to give no regard to the financial repercussions of your husband's death, trusting entirely in God or fate to provide for you. It is another thing to live one's entire life with the consequences of that early decision, with four young children to look after. My mother deeply loved and married a man who was, in the words Wallace Stevens used to describe Eliot, "too much himself." He knew exactly who he was and what he believed. By the time he was thirteen, in terms of his calling, my father already had the first intimations of his life's direction.

It must have been hard for my mother to live in the wake of a man grounded in such certainty. If my father would never define in certain terms the nature of God, he knew beyond doubt his own individual truths for living, built around a God-centered community. Sometimes it seemed my mother's mission in life to knock him off center. My older brother used to say that integrity and honesty were so deeply embedded in my father that they were a permanent state of being, that he didn't have to make a conscious decision when some opportunity arose to be self serving at the expense of others. At times, even I found that annoying in my father. When I was moving from graduate school to graduate school, and from one short-term teaching job to another, my father was more than happy to provide credit card companies with my new phone number and my new address when they called to track me down for delinquent payments.

When I complained to my father that some parents would actually side with their children against the creditors, my father was unimpressed: "You took out the loan. You pay the money."

At the same time, from my mother's point of view, there may have been something selfish in my father's decision to bring the family to Amsterdam. My father had his reasons for wanting to live in a working- class town, but that didn't mean the rest of the family necessarily shared them. Maybe my mother felt she paid a heavy price for my father's decision to move to the Mohawk Valley. As a former member of the Syracuse Junior League, she had larger social ambitions than Amsterdam could afford. She tried for awhile singing in the St. Ann's women's choir until she went head to head with the only other formally trained musician in the church, the Eastman Conservatory–educated choirmaster and organist. The choirmaster was a local guy, born and raised in Amsterdam—the brother of the Little Giants football coach. The choirmaster probably wanted to cut my mother down a notch. She probably thought of him as little league.

My mother's professional ambitions were also larger than could be contained by the traditional role of the minister's wife. She did not want to attend every altar guild meeting. She wanted her own career. By the time my younger brother Tom was three, she had started to take classes at SUNY-Albany toward the completion of her bachelor's degree. By 1968 she had completed both the B.A. and a Masters in psychology, then began to teach full-time as a lecturer at Skidmore College, in Saratoga Springs, twenty-seven miles and an entire galaxy away from working-class Amsterdam.

My mother was not alone among educated women of her generation to feel the pull of a career and the torque of the traditional role of the woman at home. She knitted beautiful sweaters, hats, and gloves for everyone in the family, and another art form she mastered we pulled up to our chins each night: For as long as I can remember she was always working on quilts. She did needlepoint, made jam from the cherries of our own trees, and pickled cucumbers from the garden. She had the touch with a rose bush. Yet she seemed to wear one hat at 253 Guy Park Avenue and another at work. Her students' image of her was radically different from what we knew of my mother at home.

One year one of my mother's Skidmore students fell in love with her—she gave my mother an honorary membership in the Society of the Officially Cool. The student's name was Betty Farber. Some weekends Betty would drive twenty-seven miles from Saratoga Springs to show up unannounced at our home. My mother was always glad to set another plate for her at dinner. Then over coffee in our living room one night, without asking any questions, Betty surprised my parents by lighting up a joint. I only know from a story my father later told that my mother stormed off to the kitchen. My father laughed and smoked it with her. When I was long out of college, I overheard my father tell his cousin that story: "That stuff doesn't work for anyone over fifty! I tried it once and didn't feel a thing!"

My mother was a petite, beautiful woman who always looked about ten years younger than her age. My father used to say that she could have any man she wanted if she ever decided to stray. Then my mother began to work on a Ph.D. in sociology from the Union Institute, a new program that finally became accredited about ten years after she completed her coursework. The program required intensive summer residencies that took my mother away from home two to three weeks at a time. My father would later tell me that many of my mother's classmates went home to their families on weekends during those residencies, but my mother stayed away. During the years she taught at Skidmore she was also often gone evenings. I had a lot of latitude at home when my father was distracted with church work, or with his own reading and writing, despite the presence of a woman my parents hired to clean and iron on weekday afternoons. Then, sometime after my grandfather died, my Grandmother Haven moved one block away to help my father at home. She often cooked for us in her apartment or at our house.

The strange thing for me is that I have almost no memory of my mother's absences. She does not talk about them. I remember only the baseball summer I spent at home with my father, and know of those other absences from what my father told me. Apparently one summer, when I must have still been in junior high, two to three weeks turned into a month or more. Maybe between my father and my grandmother my home life went on in a fairly routine way, even when my mother was gone.

Despite her occasional absences, by my sophomore year my mother had greater concern than my father that I was straying from the straight and narrow. By default or decision, my father expected self regulation. He believed in my character. He thought I would figure it out. Maybe that has made me a more independent person, but there were some treacherous early learning curves. Part of the trick of coming home late on those weekend nights was to tiptoe up the back stairs, long after my parents had fallen into a deep sleep. On a few of those nights, even in the tenth grade, I stayed out to 3 A.M. If my father heard me come in too late, he would say the next morning, "You came home a little late last night, Stephen." Then for the next few weekends I would try to arrive in my own bed closer to 1 A.M. than to 3 A.M.

If I came home too early, before midnight or so, my mother and father would sometimes be waiting up for me. My mother would call me into their bedroom, turn on the floor lamp, and examine my eyes as an ophthalmologist might, using her fingers to scissor them open as wide as they would go. We wouldn't just smoke a few joints in Brooks's basement. We'd inhale whole ounces. We'd roll up the whole bag—twenty or thirty joints—and try to smoke them all. I must have smelled to high heaven, though my parents didn't seem to notice. What my mother noticed were my eyes.

"Rev, look at him, Rev, his eyes are all red. Why are his eyes all red?"

"I drank a couple beers."

"Beer wouldn't make your eyes red like this."

"I guess I'm tired, then. But I did drink a couple beers."

"Where were you tonight? Who were you with?"

The interrogation would go on for all of ten or fifteen minutes, under the spotlight of the floor lamp. I would claim I was up at Jay Vee's Pizza Parlor and stopped for the beers on my way home. Though my parents didn't like it, by the time I was a sophomore in high school, my friends and I knew all the neighborhood pubs where we could get served. Though I was under age, my parents didn't deny me a couple of brewskies every now and then, though they preferred that I drink them at home. We were, after all, Episcopalians, and not of the teetotaling midwestern sort. As a face-saving gesture, an easy way out for them and for me, I pled guilty to the lesser public offense.

With my mother at Skidmore during the day and my father at work, in tenth and eleventh grade I skipped school with abandon whenever my friends and I felt the inclination. I could always get my father to sign an excuse for dates when I was legitimately absent. During the days I was gone, the high school would call my home. No one was there to answer the phone. The school never bothered calling my father's office or my grand-mother's apartment. We didn't own an answering machine so no tape-recorded message ever exposed me. I would handwrite the absentee ex-cuses, leaving a lot of white space between the date of some legitimate absence and the line I drew at the bottom of the page for my father's signature. After my father signed the excuse, I'd shamelessly fill in the dates when my friends and I were truant. That kept the high school happy.

Then my mother quit teaching at the beginning of my high school senior year. She was outraged that her department chair refused to rec-ognize the integrity of her Ph.D. from the unaccredited Union Institute. He wouldn't consider her a candidate for a tenure-track position. She could have remained in the department as a full-time lecturer, with a renewable contract, but instead quit in protest. She came home to start a counseling practice out of the house. She came home also to keep a better eye on my younger brother and me. My mother felt guilty for leaving the children when she worked in her academic career, and grieved for the loss of her career when she came home to the children.

With my mother home 24-7 we went to war. She began to call the high school every day to see if I had made it to homeroom on time. I responded to that challenge by refusing to attend homeroom at all until she agreed never to call again. I would go to classes but not to homeroom. As attendance was taken during that first period, I was officially absent during our standoff for two weeks or so. My father more or less got out of the way—he let my mother work it out with me. I had a taste of freedom during my sophomore and junior years and didn't want to give it back. Then my mother finally agreed to quit calling the school if I agreed never to be late for homeroom again. We called it a deal and both kept our sides of the bargain.

In order to make it to homeroom on time, I stopped smoking joints on my walk to school at 7:45 in the morning. I also never skipped school for the rest of that year, what with my mother around to answer the phone should the attendance secretary call. My mother deserves at least an assist on that one: That fall I became a straight-A student again and scored well enough on the SAT, with the added benefit of a family legacy, to get into Amherst College.

If my father never once advised me on relationships with women or how to date them, my mother was full of advice. I was in the tenth grade when I asked June Wojeski out to the movies. My mother drove me to June's house, then to the theater. Before the tires of our family Volkswagen bit June's gravel drive, my mother advised me that a man always waits until his date is seated before settling himself in. She advised me to take the young lady by the elbow, escort her to somewhere in the middle of the theater. Not too close and not too far from the screen. When she was comfortably seated I was to ask if she desired anything from the refreshment stand. Had I followed my mother's advice, June Wojeski would have either been entranced or thought I was crazy. "This is Amsterdam, New York, Mom, not *Gone with the Wind*." My mother thought that I needed to learn how to treat a lady.

On my older brother's advice, that night I took June to see *The Last Picture Show*. My mother must not have known about the "R" rating. The man behind the grated window sold the tickets to me. Cybill Shepherd goes naked in the movie, or close, and the lead, a teenage boy in small town, nowheresville Texas, ends up skipping practice to screw his basketball coach's wife. That was the last date I ever went out on with June Wojeski and just about the last time she spoke to me. Maybe my mother was on to something.

Somewhere in the mix of my mother's personal mythology, odd as it may seem coming from an old Hudson Valley family, she gave herself to the illusion of the southern, aristocratic ideal. My mother's great-grandmother was Belle Cohen, a Jewish, Georgian debutante who met my great-great-grandfather in a Saratoga Springs resort hotel shortly after the Civil War. Belle Cohen, so the story goes, became the matriarch of my mother's

New York Duchess County family. She had nine or ten granddaughters, one of them my Grandmother Harcourt. When Grandmother Harcourt gave birth to my mother, she gave her the southern *ie* rather than the *y* spelling of *Sallie*. My aunt became *Marion Belle*. Part of my mother's agenda was to turn my brothers and me into southern gentlemen, and my sister into a southern lady. In Amsterdam, New York, she had her work cut out for her.

If Woody's ex-wife Gina is to be believed, my mother found her professional niche as a counselor. Gina repeatedly told me how much my mother helped her cousin. Though my mother's counseling practice never grew very large, she had the uncanny ability to look people over in a few minutes and determine exactly what was wrong with them. She also turned those energies inward on any troubles going on in the family. Once I had left for college, I was not very often the focus of my mother's concern, but that changed when I approached thirty and was still a bachelor.

When I came home for Christmas one year, when graduate school—punctuated by periodic year-long teaching gigs—had begun to seem like a permanent lifelong condition, my mother wondered why it was that I had never seriously considered getting married. I was twenty-nine years old. She told me that afternoon that I was "no spring chicken." I had just driven home from Boston, where I was teaching as a half-time lecturer at Tufts University. I had two masters degrees under my belt, had given up on law school, and had not yet made the decision to go after a Ph.D. We were sitting in the living room of my parents' Adirondack home, the frozen Sacandaga in clear view from their picture window.

"The problem with you, Stephen, is that you get sexually involved too quickly with women, and then get so blinded by the sex that you can't ever winnow out the emotional part. You can't tell whether the women are emotionally right for you."

"*That*, Mom, is a *very* interesting topic of conversation, but I just got home for Christmas. Can we talk about something else?"

"Why don't you ever bring home the women you are dating?"

"I have. You met Maureen. You met Marina years ago."

"Yeah, but what about the rest of them?"

"You wouldn't want to meet the rest. They're not marrying material, Mom."

"Then why do you sleep with them?"

I couldn't tell my mother that I slept with them because I didn't want to marry them. Though I was not very often in those years shy of female companionship, I couldn't sleep casually with women I actually cared about. If I felt a deep, emotional bond with a physically attractive woman and then had sex with her, I would feel the stars align and start thinking of her as a lifelong mate. So maybe I stayed away from women of that sort, with whom that kind of emotional response was even a possibility. Or maybe I was holding out for the angel of my life, who never quite seemed to arrive. In any case, I wasn't ready to start working a regular nine-to-five and most women who wanted a family would have required that of me. The artistic types seemed to require less. They didn't usually want to think ahead to careers and money and children.

Things were easier if I slept with women I liked rather than loved, though I couldn't sleep with them very often without feeling guilty for violating some inner part of myself that required a spiritual bond for long-term sex. I'd sleep with them once or twice and then break the relationship off, then sleep with them again when my hormones roared and I couldn't stand it anymore: no strings attached, though only on occasion, careful to keep things open.

It was too difficult to explain to myself, much less to my mother. Why bother? Part of the trick of coming home each holiday was to have my mother focus on the problems of someone else in the family. I learned early to keep my mouth shut and duck whenever my mother's nervous insight got going. The intensity of her intelligence would fly over my shoulder and catch my sister, or one of my brothers, flush in the face.

Yet my mother loved her family deeply. She would throw herself into a medical crisis with all her energy, then collapse at home when the immediate danger passed. I remember especially my mother's homemade soups, especially the summer I came down with mono. When my sister became the third family member to face lymphoma, my mother flew to Philadelphia to cook and freeze enough dinners to last her and her husband for weeks.

Toward the end of his life, when my father was all but house-ridden and could walk no farther than to the bathroom without gasping for air, his oxygen line trailing behind him, he told me often how wonderfully my mother cared for him. What my mother lacked in constancy she made up in longevity. He could no longer walk or feed the dog. He couldn't take the garbage out. He was blind in one eye and occasionally scared everyone except my mother by going off solo in the car. He barely had the energy to lift himself into the driver's seat. My mother cooked for him, as always, but he could no longer help out by cleaning the dishes, as he so often did before. We asked her to bring in some hired help, but as always my parents worried about money. When my mother had more nursing than she could handle, she'd go up to her bedroom and shut the door, turn off the cell, and refuse to answer the land-based phone. Not even my father could call her, and he didn't have the strength to make it up the stairs.

I once saw my mother take a swing at my father. She was all of five foot four. She could hardly have hurt him. I remember seeing her try to hit him—once only—from where I was eating a bowl of Wheaties. I was sitting at the kitchen table—the one with no legs. When we moved into our Guy Park home we knocked down a wall and found a chimney right where we wanted the table to be. We built the table around that chimney—the chimney being the only leg the table needed. The kitchen door opened to the dining room, where I could see my father raise his arm to block my mother's swing.

My mother tried to hit him and she loved him. She once tore the clerical collars out of his shirts and threw them on the lawn, and loved him just the same. She went to the bishop to complain that my father was not worthy of being a minister, and loved him while she complained. In a fit of anger, she kicked the door of his car while he tried to pull out of the driveway, and loved him as he drove away. As my mother segued from one extreme of aggression to the other affectionate extreme, my father rode the waves, maintaining whatever calm he could manage. Sometimes he yelled back, more often as they aged. He was always ready to forgive her when she regained her equilibrium and gave herself more calmly to the family again.

My mother made beautiful dinners for Christmas—for all church holidays. She celebrated in our home each church season as fully as anyone. She made a quilt for each child as we headed off to college, and later for each grandchild. Love is such a strange thing. I have told my students many times that there is every reason to rejoice when one finds love, and reason also to be afraid. If one loves one will grieve: The loved one dies, even after a lifetime, or the love is betrayed, or turns out to be something utterly other than what one initially imagined.

I have told my students also—if not in these words than in so many— that you must love beyond the individual spouse. The marriage itself and beyond the marriage. Not the tree only but the energy that informs the light surge of it. You must plant olives, as Nazim Hikmet says, even if you know you will never live to see the first spread leaf. And when in some slow marathon the sprawled limbs outreach the flex of the fat trunk? When they crack deeper than the bark? That's where you tie the swing. And as you pump higher and higher still, before the arc of the sky gives way, you realize what a breeze the cant of the classroom is, and how hard the snap as you tap that sort of love into the warp and woof of a life.

At what point did my mother look out the window of our Amsterdam home, with four young children around her, and see in intimate detail a world she never would have chosen? At what point did she realize that at least some of the turbulence in and around her would follow her wherever she chose to go?

My sister left for boarding school when I was in the sixth grade, my older brother for the Deerfield Academy when I was in the seventh. Though my brother would come back to Amsterdam for two high school years, he would eventually repeat his junior year and spend three of five secondary school years away from home in private academies. That left me as the oldest child at 253 Guy Park Avenue. My role was to be a bridge between the older children and my younger brother Tom. My role was to calm my mother down. My role was to have no complaints—in school, playing ball, with money, or with my friends—that I would ever need to share with anyone. It was a high-wire act. I embraced it with a passion. I thought I could handle anything.

My father eventually handpicked the colleges to which I applied and drove me to the interviews. I needed that sort of guidance as I had never heard of St. Lawrence University, or Hamilton or Hobart College. Only one other member of the Koller 49ers ever chased an undergraduate degree. I don't know if the violence outside our home fueled some of the turbulence in it. Maybe it is a kind of violence not to be able to listen to a concert, or to a poetry reading—not to be able to talk about real literature, or art, among the townspeople to whom you have given the better part of your life. Maybe my father seemed impossible to nudge off-center, his sense of home having little to do with any specific locale. Give him a study, a bunch of books, a church community, and a family, and he was there, counting his blessings, warming the youngest of his children before the fire.

In junior high I sometimes thought of escaping to boarding school. I thought ahead to college. Then I gave myself to the wildness swirling everywhere around me. How could I ever hold it against my mother that she left so briefly, dreamed however momentarily of a life beyond the man she married, and then could never, ever let go of the shock that turned out to be home?

8

Legacy

Frank lost his virginity to Carla Tucci. We called her Bozo. She had curly, black, frizzy hair, somewhat of an Orphan Annie cut, terrible acne, a red bulbous nose, and was grossly overweight. She was fourteen years old. Frank had just turned fifteen. He had no romantic interest in her whatsoever. She lived next door to John Ripepi. When we played basketball, we could see her and her younger brothers and sisters playing on the swing set in their yard. Her grandparents, who could speak no English, lived right across the street, on the other side of Tryon. I don't know how anyone figured out she was game. She first started giving the older kids in the neighborhood blow jobs, in groups of three or four. Then Frank and Steven DiBacco wanted in. Frank would call out to her from Rat Ripepi's yard,

"Carla, how you feeling today, Carly?"

"Okay, Frankie, I'm okay!"

"Good enough for a blow job today, Carly?"

"Oh, Frankie! Stop it, Frankie!"

She would blush deep enough to match the permanent color of her nose and hurry back inside while Frank cracked up laughing. We cracked up laughing at Frank—that he was crazy enough to say right out in the open what she and every one of us knew. She would let him take her down to the river, or would let him into her house when her parents and the other Tucci children weren't at home.

I lagged behind the surge in Frank's new body. A year younger than Frank, I hadn't hit my growth spurt yet. In the fall of ninth grade puberty had barely begun for me. I yearned after girls like anyone else but hadn't yet learned to imagine having sex with them. I only imagined having sex with the nudes in magazines we kept hidden in a large plastic bag, beneath the stacked firewood, on the side of our back porch. As for real girls, before

I met Mary, the one girlfriend I ever cared for was Judy Tambasco, love of my elementary and junior high school life. I lost her somewhere in the black hole of middle school when she insisted that I begin to walk her home. I didn't really consider her offer. My friends would have crucified me.

I fell in love with Judy Tambasco when I was the new kid in third grade. I knew it the minute I saw her: thick, long, wavy black hair, soft black-brown eyes, skin like snow in July, a button nose. Soon it was mutual. We confirmed it through our friends, wrote each other's names on our pencil boxes and on our erasers. All of this meant that we never said a word to one another. One look from Judy Tambasco stopped me dead in my tracks. I wouldn't throw a snowball at a truck in front of her. I could barely speak to anyone when she was near me, though she was sometimes my partner when we squared up to dance in gym class. The teacher would actually line the boys and girls up and make the boys choose. That was the moment of truth. Sometimes I looked for a safe out by picking one of the quiet, unpopular girls. Whenever I picked Judy, the Greek chorus of my entire class chimed in till they could actually see purple blood pulse in my veins.

At Theodore Roosevelt Junior High, Judy and I shared many of the same classes, but we exchanged ID bracelets only through the intermediary of one of her friends, and gave the bracelets back in the same way, without ever actually talking it over. Our silent, never openly acknowledged commitment to one another lasted nearly seven years. Then Judy wanted to take it to the next level, which probably required that I recognize her as an actual breathing being by speaking with her on occasion, by spending time together. She was still a goddess to me. Maybe I was scared of measuring up to her angelic standard, or maybe I feared betraying my friends, especially Frank, both of us wary of any commitment that might trump a known and tested quantity, our blood brotherhood.

Anyone who walked home with me would have also walked with Frank, and with Rat and Joe Battaglia, Overbaugh, and Mark DiCaprio. That was not an either/or situation. It was both or nothing. It would have been a different me, with Frank and the others gunning for Judy, firing squirt guns or snowballs at us, or knocking books out of her hands and mine, just to see whether my true loyalties were with the guys. With Mary on the phone I could say anything, and nothing Frank could do or say would ever shock her. With Judy? She wore little white ankle socks with a black skirt, black dress shoes, and a white blouse, complete with frills around the sleeves. She seemed kind. She was pretty. We walked the same direction home, just short of a mile from school. She lived three blocks away from me, further into the West End. Her father ran an insurance agency. My friends would have sung to us all the way down Division Street till I sang back to them. I wasn't up for the complexity. We stuck to Guy Park and conceded Division to the girls. I didn't want Judy to descend to earth only to find a tar baby stuck in clay. With one touch I would have stuck her there, too. Whatever divinity I attributed to her, she clearly didn't want it. When I was with her, it wasn't so much that I felt her watching me. With Judy anywhere nearby, some larger part of me took pains to watch myself.

One night during the summer before ninth grade, a bunch of us took bedrolls and sleeping bags out on Rat's court and played basketball until it got dark. After we spent all the money we had on soda and chips, we were ready to call it a night, but Frank didn't want the party to end. He had done some yard work for an elderly couple near my house and knew they kept cases of beer on their screened-in porch. Bean—we called Mark DiCaprio *Bean*—and Frank and I sneaked up to the screen door. It was too dark to see. Frank went in and found it: a case of Ballantine Ale. He handed two six-packs to Bean and one to me. We ran back down to Rat's house. I remember thinking it tasted like perfume. I have a special affection, now, for Ballantine Ale, a shared personal history. I drank a can or two before we all went to sleep.

Sometime around two or three in the morning we heard some screaming up on Division, half a block away. When we finally woke up enough to realize who was making all the noise and ran up the block, we found Frank, hanging on to the lifeline of some lady's front porch railing, while some older teenage kid in a muscle shirt and shorts kept trying to drag him by one leg down the porch stairs. The house was built right up to the sidewalk, like most houses on the street—no yard, neighbors on either side a few feet away. Lights were coming on. Frank kept kicking at the older kid with his free leg. Then the kid let go, smacked Frank twice in the head, and grabbed him by the collar. Frank held on, swearing at the teenager all the while and yelling for us to jump in. Bean and I kept our distance. The teenage kid was big.

The lady, out on the porch in a bathrobe, seemed to be taking Frank's side: "Get outta here! Leave him alone! Call the police! Someone call the police!" Frank called him a fucking asshole. The guy in the muscle shirt hit Frank one more time, this time with his open hand. Then he walked down Division, jumped into an old Pontiac where his girl was waiting, and drove off. Frank was yelling and crying and laughing, all at once: "Where the fuck were you guys, ya bunch of chickenshits? We could have kicked his ass! We could have taken him!"

By now Bean was laughing, "Fucking Frankie!" The police pulled up. We headed back down to Rat's court. When Frank tried to slip off, the woman grabbed him by the arm and said, "Oh, no you don't." She knew Frank from the neighborhood and phoned Mrs. Johnson. Frank didn't tell the police much—he claimed the kid started hitting him for no reason—but Mary, Frank's mother, got the truth out of him. Frank kept drinking when the rest of us went to sleep and then decided to go for a walk. The teenage kid was parked with his girlfriend and already had her shirt off by the time Frank found them. When the kid looked up, his mouth on her breast, and found the moon of Frank's original smiley smeared against his backseat window, some primal reflex went off. The teenager cornered him on the lady's porch. Frank started yelling, ringing her doorbell and pounding the walls. That was only the beginning of Frank's local legacy.

There was a sweetness in Frank that adolescence couldn't entirely knock out of him. Another night, over for dinner at Frank's with Bean Dicaprio, we grilled a couple of chuck steaks. No one else was home. Frank was laughing about one thing or the other, fooling around. Then he said, for no apparent reason, "Just never hit me right here when I'm laughing," and pointed to his solar plexus and couldn't stop laughing. Bean, who was by then a running back for the freshman team, reached over and smacked Frank lightly in the solar plexus. Frank threw up all over the floor. Then we were all three of us down on the floorboards, only one of us to clean up the mess.

Still another moment, when Frank was seventeen and I was sixteen: spring of our sophomore year. June 1973. Though I had my license for all of three months, my father agreed to trust us on a road trip to Boston with his Toyota Corolla under one condition: We were not allowed to drive at night. We accepted that condition even as we had no intention of letting a curfew veto a late night's fun. My sister was spending her college summer in Cambridge. Frank's brother Billy, having just graduated from high school, was trying to decide whether to apply to college or to join the army. He had a room in an apartment near Kenmore Square. One Friday afternoon we drove the two hundred miles east to visit them.

After drinking a few beers and smoking a couple of joints in Billy's apartment, we decided to go out on the town. When I reached into my pocket, no keys! We found them hanging from the ignition. The car was locked. Toyota Corollas had locks that flipped open like small doors— almost impossible to hook and pull open with a coat hanger slipped through the rubber seal of the car window. In the streamlined logic of three wasted teenagers, we realized almost instantly the only reasonable thing to do: We had to kick out one of the rear windows. Billy backed up a few feet, took a running jump and missed, denting my father's back door with the heel of a cowboy boot.

"The Old Rev's sure not going to like that one," he said, the two brothers laughing.

Billy and Frank always called my father "The Old Rev," except when my father was around. Then they called him Mr. Haven. A couple of passersby who saw Billy's miss took a hard look at our plates. "It's our car," we assured them. They shook their heads. Though we were in Boston, one of them said, "Only in New York!" as Billy wound up for a second try. Even I believed for an instant in the inevitability of having to dropkick my father's car window. But the dented door took it to another level.

"Wait a minute, Billy, you're kicking my father's car!"

"The Old Rev won't mind."

"Actually, I think he *would* mind, Billy!" I was on board with taking the window out, but I was pissed about the dented door.

"What do you want, Stephen, the soft touch for The Old Rev?"

"Just don't kick the fucking door!"

"All right, all right, Stephen! Everything's okay here."

"It's just a car, Harc!" Frank said, wanting to fan the fire. "If someone doesn't take that window out in a minute, I'm going to take it out myself."

"Is that right, Frank? *You're* going to kick my car?"

Then we found a piece of broken brick in the gutter. Billy gave the window a few sharp taps. The glass cracked and crazed. We pushed the window through and brushed off the backseat, then went out to a bar where Billy knew the bouncers didn't check IDs. All night long, Frank and Billy chanted their newfound mantra:

"The soft touch for The Reverend! Have another beer, Harc! Have another beer, Stephen! The soft touch for The Old Rev."

Frank and I made it back to my sister's apartment that night after dropping Billy at his place. The next morning the Toyota was gone from where we parked it. For at least a minute it seemed to have vanished. We were stunned. It simply disappeared.

"Who'd want to steal that freaking piece of shit?"

"Yeah, well, you wanted to drive in it last night."

"Yeah, but it's got a broken window."

"Funny. *Very* funny, Frank. What if it was Douglass's car?" I had started to call Frank's stepfather Douglass. "Who'd be joking around then?"

Then we noticed the mouth of a driveway next to where we had left the car. Who would have known, what with two high-rise apartment buildings on either side? It took us a couple of hours to track down the Toyota. We borrowed seventy-five dollars from my sister to pay for the tow and the fine. That afternoon we finally headed out to the Mass. Pike for the three-and-a-half hour drive back to upstate New York. When we pulled across the bridge into Amsterdam, Frank said,

"Amsterdam sure is a shit hole."

"Yup, sure is."

Frank thought about that one for a minute or more, his regional loyalties kicking in:

"Yeah, well, but not even Boston can beat our supermarkets!"

The clincher, the epitome of Frank's local legacy came early, when he was
still fifteen, the day Carla Tucci's grandmother, yelling at him in Italian,
chased him out of the Tucci home, hitting him over the head with a broom,
his pants down around his shins. The old woman was tough. She chased
him up and down Tryon Street, shaking the broom over her head. Frank
kept falling down, with one arm up to block her swings, the other working
at his pants. Frank's mother Mary would always call him "John Franklin
Johnson" whenever she was getting serious. That was a John Franklin
Johnson day. When the police had left, when the Tuccis dropped the whole
matter, and each set of parents agreed to watch more closely their son, their
daughter, Mary softened: "I understand, Frankie, why you would want to
sleep with your girlfriend, but with a girl you don't even care about? With
that girl?"

I can only wonder, in horror, as the father of a teenage daughter, what
Carla Tucci might say if we were to ask her, these years later, her opinion
of Frank and me, Rat, Joe Battag, Steven DiBacco, Bean, and Donny O.

9

Luisa

Sometimes I wonder whether it was all that much different, Frank's rush to initiate himself into adolescence through the premature embrace of Carla Tucci, and my embrace of Maria Luisa over Judy Tambasco. Blow jobs weren't enough for Frank. He was fifteen. He had to get laid. Just to see. For me, Mary didn't seem to be a choice. She was a gift from the gods, or at least from Donny Overbaugh. She simply happened to me, in fate, in the drift of things. I didn't see her again after that first date, for nearly two years, though we kept talking on the phone. Eventually she transferred into the public high school when she was a sophomore and I was a junior. That's when it really began to happen. We kept talking even when she started dating the two-years-older-than-me Mike Pesce. I later came to know Pesce during my summer pumping gas on the New York State Thruway. By then, we were both Mary's ex-boyfriends.

Mike Pesce drove a 1963 Plymouth Valiant, a stick shift that did so well on gas that our tips from the thruway station kept it going. The summer after my junior year, we would put a couple bucks in the Valiant, then head up with a cooler of beer to swim and camp in the Adirondacks. Of course Mike and I traded notes. It was a sort of bond between us that we were both Mary's ex-boyfriends. Mary slept with him when she was in the ninth grade. When we started dating she let me know that she had every intention of having sex with me. But Mary was particular. She would only go so far in Brooks's basement. It would never happen there in the fullest sense. It wouldn't happen outdoors. We had to wait for the right moment, in her house or mine, when no one was home.

It happened in my bedroom. I don't remember where my parents and younger brother were. My older brother was off in boarding school, my sister at Vassar College. I remember thinking *It looks just like Playboy!* and wanting her to leave when almost instantly it was over. Before it was over, she said, "You're killing me, *killing me!*" and later laughed with her sisters, with me on the phone, about how I kept trying to drive up the wrong hole.

The year I went away to college Mary became pregnant with Jimmy Fassio's baby. She was seventeen. Jimmy was nineteen. That was the same year Bucky Hart got Mary's younger sister pregnant when she was just fifteen. Mary's father and older brother powwowed with the Hart and Fassio families: two shotgun weddings. Mary was a beautiful girl—thin waist, petite, the longest hair I'd ever seen, nothing but confidence in her slight breasts, in her whole body. She had a little bit of dark hair on her upper lip, which my friends made into a moustache through their tendency to exaggerate everything. I think we made love three times, if we count the first misfire, once in my house, twice in hers. That she was so particular was my saving grace. Maybe that was one reason she threw me over for the older Jimmy—she needed to make love to her boyfriend. I didn't have an apartment. I didn't have a car.

Pumping gas on the New York State Thruway, Mike Pesce waxed nostalgic over Mary. I made it a duet. That was the summer before my senior year. I hadn't found anyone else who would sleep with me. I thought, mistakenly, that I would have to wait until I went away to college.

For years after I left Amsterdam, I continued to run into Mary whenever I came home from Amherst College, and later from the University of Iowa—Christmas and summer vacations. She worked in the Amsterdam mall as a cashier in one of the discount clothes stores that faced the escalator. I couldn't as much as breathe for a minute in that mall before Mary would know I was there. If I just walked on by she would yell out, "All right, then, *don't* say hello. *Be* a stranger! Just walk on by." If I stopped to say hello, she'd say, "Jimmy will kill me if he sees me!" One time I ran into both of them at the A&P. Mary, never shy of words, dropped her eyes and studied the floorboards, blushing, half smiling. Jimmy said hello. Jimmy and I were teammates for a season on the high school soccer team. Another time, from behind the cashier's counter, Mary asked to meet me for a cup of coffee when she got off work. She didn't show.

One winter when I was still a graduate student at the University of Iowa, Mary's friend had rented an apartment in a house directly across from my parents' home. That Christmas she kept calling my parents' number. My mother kept telling her, "Stephen's got a girlfriend, Mary. Her name is Maureen." She wanted to see me anyway, across the street, at her friend's apartment, 9 P.M. Curiosity got the best of me. When I came in, the stereo was going. She asked me if I noticed something. It was "our song." Something from Led Zeppelin, probably, though I can't even now remember and certainly didn't remember then. She was thin as always. She looked good. As if our lives expressed themselves only in detail, she knew my birthday and the birthdays of my two brothers. Even my sister's, though she had never even met her. We sat there for a few awkward moments, maybe twenty minutes, maybe thirty. When I said I had better go, she walked me to the door, kissed me, and stuck her tongue down my throat. Jimmy had his hands full.

I later heard through Woody or Murph or someone that Mary had an affair. For a while, Jimmy moved out of the house Mary's parents had given them. The two kids stayed with their mother. They had all been living next door to Mary's childhood home, two households, two generations of an Italian family in a Puerto Rican neighborhood, on the last street in Amsterdam. Then Jimmy moved back in.

I find myself wishing, from time to time, that I actually loved the girl I first made love to, though maybe I do, if I didn't then. I can't quite believe that Mary was to me only what Carla Tucci was to Frank. Mary is still with Jimmy, as far as I know, and Frank has been married to Vel, his one wife for over twenty-five years, whatever that might say about their capacity for love and loyalty and longevity. My own first marriage barely made it past a ten-year anniversary.

That night in Russo's Bar and Grill, over meatball sandwiches and beer, Woody told me what happened to Mary's son after he had grown. Shortly after he graduated from high school, in his parents' bedroom he tucked the end of his father's magnum in his mouth and became a child again. Almost unimaginable to me, what Mary must have seen, the silkscreen of her son's head against the wall of that most intimate of human rooms, so that, in an instant, the mother melded back into the child. Almost unimaginable, the two of them slumped against the floor, beyond any thought or reason, as if Mary were kneeling at the altar of the only bedroom that would ever fully master her.

They scrubbed the blood off, patched the wall, painted it, and for a while continued to call it home because they could afford no other. I was relieved, in college, and all the more relieved now, that it was Jimmy—not me—who had fathered Mary's baby. I never met her son, but thought of him often when I was away that first year at Amherst College: "She's married now, and swollen to the brim / and forced, in youth, a woman's role to play." Fragments from a bad sonnet I wrote in freshman English. The closing couplet sticks in my head still: "How was it that she knew, and I could not / Foretell, the counter lots our lives had wrought?"

I spent the rest of that week thinking of Mary and her son. I kept wondering if I would run into her, in the laundromat, in The Armory Grill, in Russo's Bar. Jimmy would have had a fit if I'd ever directly contacted her, if only to say "I'm sorry," as if my quiet witness to the trouble swirling in and around me could mean much of anything. I did my laundry down in the East End, just to see what chance might bring. Each dark, petite, long-haired woman, each Italian, each Puerto Rican, morphed into Mary when she turned her back to me.

10

The Ax

Early that Wednesday afternoon, before I had dinner with Woody at Russo's Bar, while I was poking around Woody's old neighborhood, I stopped by to catch a glimpse of Brooks's basement apartment. I didn't approach the house, much less the door. I took the corner off Wall Street onto Greene, parked the car, and stared for a full ten or fifteen minutes at concrete stairs that led down a bank along the side of Brooks's old house. At the bottom of those steps, a door opened into the basement. Maybe because I was a father of two by then—soon to be a stepfather of four more—it looked almost sinister to me, the last house on a dead-end street. The houses in the neighborhood seemed to sag to one side or the other— each one a face with an eye absent from one gaping socket. Brooks's house seemed, even more fully, to reinvent the rules for gravity and geometry. I wasn't foolish enough to knock on the door to say hello. Whoever might have answered would have thought I was out of my mind. His mother and brother didn't know who I was, even back then, though I was in their home—in their basement—almost every single winter high school weekend for nearly three years running.

Brooks's mother—more than slightly overweight, long black hair, thick face, a hard drinker with her own weekend party always going on— didn't know, and didn't want to know, half of the other kids who cranked her basement stereo till 2 or 3 A.M. When she could stand no more, she'd flip the main, pitching us into a black silence punctuated only by the sound of smashing glass. Whenever it went dark, Brooks started hurling beer bottles off the walls. He threw them right across the room. I don't know why he smashed those bottles in the dark. Maybe he was trying to tell his mother something. Maybe he was mad at her or at all of us, or more likely at those of us who wandered down from elsewhere—the West End or Pollack Hill.

83

Either way, it made Frank angry to think that one of those bottles might catch him or me in the face when we couldn't be looking. We made a pact between us—if ever Brooks attacked one of us, the other would jump in. Murph and Woody had known Brooks since Day One. Frank and I knew enough to keep him always in our peripheral vision.

I got out of the car and walked down Wall to Union Street again. The Annex was shut down, though I still felt Brooks sitting at the bar. When I was in undergraduate school, he lived with his wife in the apartment above the pub. The last time I sat in The Annex with him, Brooks asked the bartender to put the Playboy station on. Then he heard his wife's foot on the stairs and yelled, "Quick! Change the station!" I knew right then that he cared about something.

One of my earliest memories—my first trouble with Brooks—was in junior high, when I worked the only paper route I could find—for the *Schenectady Times Gazette* rather than for the local and more lucrative *Amsterdam Recorder*. My route was up and down Union, right past Lorenzo's and Luba's Tavern, past Woody's and Murph's houses. Brooks was one of the three or four kids who ripped the newspaper bag off my shoulder, twisted it around my arms as I tried to pull away, and started throwing punches. I didn't know who the other kids were, but someone began to yell, "At least give him a chance to get the bag off!" By then I was already on the ground. Brooks got a couple kicks in. He must have been twelve or thirteen years old. I wasn't hurt much. I didn't even tell my parents, but I was scared to death to deliver the papers, much less collect on Fridays. On Fridays, the anxiety of announcing my presence in the neighborhood by ringing every *Times Gazette* doorbell fought it out with my desire to get paid until I hit the corner where Union emptied into Major Lane. For weeks, I tried to do what I thought was the only honorable thing. Frank Johnson came with me on the afternoon that Woody arranged for me to fight Brooks, one-on-one. At that time, I knew Woody only from baseball. I waited for a good half hour in an empty lot, with Frank as my back up. No one showed. I don't believe for a second Brooks was afraid. One-on-one wasn't his style.

Brooks's basement consisted of four rooms and a subcellar. The basement door opened to the main room, where we kept our kegs. The walls were fake wood paneling. There was an orange spray-painted oven—not a gas heater, but a regular gas oven. We lit it and left the oven door open. That kept us warm enough, even in January, even during blizzards that hit the Mohawk Valley with a force and regularity we never even thought to question and almost actually welcomed. The room we usually partied in was off the main one, in the back, a door frame only separating one room from another, no doors in between. Brooks kept to himself or hung out in the front room with his three closest friends—Nappy, Czerew, and Ross—smoking a cigar and manning the keg. The back room had a couple of old couches and an armchair. The room off to the right of the main we hardly ever used, except when one of us had a girlfriend along. There was a couch and an armchair and no light.

I remember taking Mary into that dark room on one of the rare nights she agreed to come to Brooks's apartment. She let me touch her breasts and let me slide my fingers down inside the slick wonder of her jeans. So things wouldn't get out of hand she insisted on keeping her belt buckled. There were six or seven guys partying in the rest of the apartment with one of Mary's friends. They usually left alone whoever slipped off with a girl to the dark, but Gary Czerew must have been trashed that night. He kept coming in with a table lamp, held lanternlike over his head.

"What the fuck is going on in here, Harc? You been in here a fucking hour! You get lost in there or something? What are you, a champion or something?"

The fourth room, by the subcellar, was barely large enough to contain the apartment's one refrigerator, spray-painted orange like the stove. There was no bathroom in the entire basement apartment. We peed out the door. The yard, such it was, was on a slant. The concrete slab outside the basement door ran downhill. I can't begin to imagine the quantity of urine we washed down that slab those late-night weekends! Brooks hosed the whole thing off on Saturday and Sunday mornings. In winter he'd use buckets of hot water. The few girls who ever came to those parties must have asked Brooks, or his sister Theresa, to use the bathroom on the house's first floor. Maybe Brooks let the girls into his home to pee to be nice to them, in a way he never would have allowed any of the guys. He was half crazy and going nowhere, and knew it, and the girls knew it too, and some of them liked him just the same, maybe for that very reason.

Brooks was a muscular, thick-bodied five foot five, with long blond hair down to his butt. The joke among the kids who had known him forever from Union Street was that he looked like Cousin Itt from *The Addams Family*. He was about as talkative. Some Saturdays he used to drink a case of quarts by day—twelve of them, Ballantine Ale—to warm up for that night's keg. He wouldn't go near pot or anything hallucinogenic—none of his closest friends would, except Ross, all of them a year younger than Murph and Woody, Frank and Rod and me. Brooks also didn't much go for hard rock, though he conceded the turntable to the rote, ear-shattering, monochromatic mania of Murph, probably because Brooks didn't care all that much what we listened to, or because he loved Murph like a brother, or like a cousin anyway. Still, he and Nap and Czerew were suckers for Creedence Clearwater Revival, a sign of intelligence, I thought, when the other options were Kiss and Aerosmith. In some of our better moments, not on nights when there were big parties but on slow winter afternoons, though Brooks couldn't sing, I more than once heard him croon "Bad Moon Rising" and "Proud Mary" with Nappy and Czerew. It was hard to figure. Frank thought they sounded like a bunch of hillbillies:

> I hear hurricanes a-blowing.
> I know the end is coming soon.
> I fear rivers overflowing.
> I hear the voice of rage and ruin.

> Hope you got your things together.
> Hope you are quite prepared to die.
> Looks like we're in for nasty weather.
> One eye is taken for an eye.

Sometimes I'd sing along with them, and Brooks would bite on a stogie and say, "You're funny as hell, Harc, funny as hell." Or even more enigmatically, as a sort of refrain that he would use for any occasion requiring him to recognize my presence in the room, he'd say, "A lot of rebounds, Harc, a *lot* of rebounds!" That was something he started saying after watching our first few basketball games. Otherwise he wouldn't say much to me. But he'd sing:

> Left a good job in the city
> Workin' for the man ev'ry night and day
> And I never lost one minute of sleepin',
> Worrin' 'bout the way things might have been.

> Cleaned a lot of plates in Memphis
> Pumped a lot of pain down in New Orleans,
> But I never saw the good side of the city,
> Till I hitched a ride on the riverboat queen.

> If you come down to the river,
> Bet you gonna find some people who live.
> You don't have to worry 'cause you have no money,
> People on the river are happy to give.

It was, after all, a river town.

This is how it would go with Brooks, though it didn't happen often. A kid comes in to buy some pot in the cabin fever of a Saturday, winter afternoon. There are four or five of us in Brooks's basement, which by now is as much our own hangout as it is Brooks's home. We come and go as we please, even if Brooks is not there. On this day we have come early: Frank, Murph, Woody, and me, and Brooks makes five. The kid makes six. He is one or two years younger than us, six feet tall or so: a deerskin, light-brown, leather jacket with a row of tassels hanging down from his chest. A Jesse Collins Young type, a Crosby, Stills, and Nash, without the added *duende* of Neil Young, but still the Black Elf encounters him, or he encounters *it*, when, uninvited, he knocks on the door, having heard somewhere that he could buy some pot here.

Though no one exactly knows him, we offer to sell him the pot he's after, twenty dollars an ounce, two for thirty-five. Brooks has been pacing around all afternoon with a thick walking stick—gnarled branch of a tree, nothing finished or polished, an inch and a half in diameter, about the size of a cane. He moves off to one of the back rooms, saying nothing, flipping the stick in the air and catching it again, end over end. The kid sits down on the couch near the door, next to Murph and Woody, with Frank and me leaning against one wall. Brooks has never smoked pot in his life, much less sold it. If he cares that we hide ounces behind a poster, in a hole in one of his walls, whenever we go home, he has never said a word. Neither does he say anything to Jesse Collins during the entire twenty minutes the boy is in the basement. Murph leans in Woody's direction to whisper something in his ear, and Brooks makes a clean shot from across the room. For no reason that I can ever imagine, he flicks the stick as a college kid might a Frisbee, elbow close to his side, forearm extended at a forty-five-degree angle. For weeks afterward he keeps saying, as if it were the buzzword for everyone's wild laughter, "No more two for thirty-five!" That's it. No further explanation. "No more two for thirty-five!" as if he were sick and tired of the way everyone was cheating us, though no one ever was.

The stick catches the kid above his right eye. Blood breaks from the gash. Brooks goes back to his beer and cigar and stands there watching, silently, as if he had nothing to do with it—voyeur, rubberneck. Woody rips his own shirt off, wraps it tight around the kid's head, and walks him the one block out to Wall Street, where he stops a car. Murph keeps saying, more to himself than to anyone else, "Oh, my God, Brooks! Oh, my God!" A stunned silence sets in. I don't say a thing, slipping into my usual veneer of calm and quiet, the wall of an inner room to which I almost habitually retreat, then as now, when things begin to swirl. Then Frank starts yelling, "You crazy Fuck, Brooks! You crazy son-of-a bitch," pacing back and forth as if he's about to hit him. Even Woody doesn't know what to say when he comes back in. Another nervous silence sets in. Then Brooks says, "No more two for thirty-five!" quietly, almost beneath his breath, and everyone starts laughing. *No more two for thirty-five?!* On the way back home that evening, Frank and I renew our pact, and I wonder, tossing all night long, why I laughed and why it was Woody, not me, who jumped so quickly to wrap that boy's head.

Brooks never went to school beyond the sixth grade, though my guess is he never went often even before then, and his mother didn't force him. He met Nappy, Ross, and Czerew at the Academy Street Elementary School, where Woody and Murph were a year ahead of him. Whether truancy alone first landed him in juvenile court, I don't know. Before long it was a series of foster homes. Brooks was fourteen by the time I started hanging out with him, though I had that one earlier, never-acknowledged encounter. Maybe the law had given up on him. By the time he was fourteen, there were no more truant officers, no more foster homes. Whatever authorities there were let him stay with his mother, where he kept to himself and started working underage in one of the factories as soon as they would take him.

Every now and then Brooks would talk about the hicks he was forced to live with—how one foster father kept trying to make him clean the barn. If there was one thing in the world he refused to do, it was shovel shit. He used to punch cows square in the forehead, hard as he could: *dumb fucks, couldn't feel a thing!* In lighter moments, he would take off his shoes and socks to laugh at the marvel of his own prehistoric anatomy: He had webbed toes, *and I can't even freakin' swim!* He used to lay on his back, lift his two legs in the air as a women might fit into stirrups for a gynecological exam, and hold a match to his butt. The flamethrower of his farts made his old buddies laugh. *That one burnt the hair off my ass!* Nap and Czerew and Ross would egg him on to brew up another one again. Brooks would eventually work in one of the West End mills, about a half an hour by foot away. He became a material cutter in one of the leather factories. He married the younger sister of a girl who went to Clara S. Bacon Elementary with me.

Here is another moment, the last time I saw Brooks lose his head. It is January or February and snowing hard outside. There is no keg this evening, but the refrigerator in the back room is packed with bottles of Genesee

Cream Ale, and other cases are waiting in the snow. Everyone has at least twenty-four bottles of Genny except me, as I have never been able to drink more than twelve. Someone has hidden some pot in the subcellar of the basement, the door of which is near the refrigerated beer. Ross goes into the subcellar to bring the bag out at nine or ten, maybe eleven o'clock that evening. I don't know why anyone else would have a reason to go back there. Before that night, I have only been in the subcellar once or twice. You need a flashlight to see: hard earthen floor, joists and floorboards overhead, bricks and cinder blocks, cobwebs and a lot of dust. I think it is Richard Podowski who comes back to say "There's a fucking turd back there!" Brooks never even goes in to look. Pretty soon everyone starts yelling, "Who laid that turd down? Who lay that baby down!? Whose got the shit-stained BVDs?" I think it is Abu, always the instigator, always trying to rile everyone up, who starts yelling, "Ross, you shitter! Pull his pants down! We know you've got the brown on your BVDs!"

I don't know if Abu has anything to do with the turd that is plainly back there, as by now everyone but Brooks has gone in to take a look. No one cares that Brooks has, many times before, kicked his German shepherd back into the subcellar to calm him down, what with the crowd and the noise. Ross, proverbial drughead, an alcoholic by the time he turns eighteen, is conscious enough on that night to mumble, "Not me, man, not me!" By then I am yelling along with everyone else, "Ross, you shitter! Get the shovel out!" I don't know if we are just drunk and stoned or on THC that night—little pink barrels—or mescaline, which in either case amounts to the same thing, both of them probably strychnine—a good cheap buzz if we drink enough. I don't know how long all of us ride Ross.

I didn't know where it was going, and still don't know exactly what happened, except that I was a part of it. It was a turning point for me. It was the start of my desire to leave. I had felt it before, in junior high school, when for a few weeks I feared Ervin Garcia taunting me for quarters. That earlier desire to escape Amsterdam was in my mind, or in my heart, and was a fear of someone or something other than myself. This was in my marrow.

All night that night I lay awake, and for years afterward I wondered at my role in the near-violence of that evening. The crowd, the mob, a handful of teenage kids, singled out an innocent to take a hit, and I was one voice in the choir of their urging. I never knew exactly why I harassed Ross to the point that someone else attacked him, but I know I thought about it longer than the rest of my friends. Maybe, once Abu had picked Ross to take the fall, I jeered with the rest of them in case they might change their collective minds and single me as the odd man out, as I was in actuality more truly than Ross, given the state of things—where my family had been, where I was going. Maybe I knew instinctively that something was going to happen and said, with the rest of them, *Let it be him rather than me*, the chants of *shitter* and *shit-ass* crescendoing until Brooks exploded with the ax. I had never noticed it before, leaning against the refrigerator.

Brooks started swinging wildly at Ross, missing him by a foot or less with each wedged crack in the couch's pinewood frame. Ross slid down further on the couch with each missed swing. Woody grabbed Brooks from behind, hugged him for a minute or more, the way one might hold a child, and cooed to him, somewhere beyond the reach of reason. He called him *John* and then *Johnny*. "Put it down, John. Put it down, Johnny." Brooks let the ax drop to the floor. Woody picked it up, took it outside, and hid it in the yard. Brooks went off to the one dark room and stayed there a long while. Ross kept saying, "Not me, man, not me!" and didn't leave. Only Abu was still yelling, "You shitter, Ross! Get the shovel!" For years, then, any time Ross screwed up, in any possible way, someone called out, as if it were a joke, "Get the ax, Brooks! Get the ax!"

11

PK

As long as I lived in Amsterdam, though I didn't often say anything, I took offense at the way my friends and their parents occasionally poked fun at my father and his profession. When I was in elementary school, I didn't know what to say in his defense and couldn't understand why they wouldn't implicitly respect such a wonderful man. My father would play chess with me and my younger brother Tom, or after church would simply read whole Sundays away in our living room, breaking only for dinner and cocktails in the evening, or to feed a rip-roaring, day-long fire. We always kept a fire burning those winter weekends and winter evenings. When we moved into our Victorian on Guy Park Avenue in 1965, the house was nearly seventy years old. No one worried about a lined chimney back then. My father built a blazer, the first cold day. He was the force behind those fires.

Now I think my father's displeasure with the title *Reverend* wasn't simply a matter of proper nomenclature. He didn't like to be singled out in public. He didn't like to be viewed as different from the other guys, though he was plainly different, as any one could see, if only in the form of his clerical collar. I was forty-five years old before I was given the full story. My father, as a young clergyman in Binghamton, New York, winced at the tendency of his parishioners to call him by what he considered to be an inappropriate title, so he decided to take things into his own hands. In order to correct matters, my father wrote a note in the church bulletin explaining that *Reverend* is a written and not a spoken title. From that day on he became *Rev* to my mother. Even in my childhood church, at the after-service coffee hour, my mother would call out to him across a crowded room, "Oh, Rev! I'll see you back at the house. I'm going now."

Robert Marshall Haven, circa 1989. Courtesy of
St. Ann's Episcopal Church, Amsterdam, New York.

My mother was the only person in the entire galaxy who could call him *Reverend*—or anything close—without getting a grimace out of him. That was their old source of affection. Frank and Billy got a laugh out of it. That is how he became, in their eyes and in the eyes of my other friends, "the Old Reverend," or for short, "the Old Rev."

I was also forty-five years old before my father told me that he was required as a boy to wear a coat and tie every time he came to the dinner table. That explained something. My grandparents had a live-in, black maid, though my grandmother worked right along beside her, in a large, beautiful home in Loudonville, New York, a suburb of Albany. My grandfather was an executive accountant for Bell Telephone. He was the president of the Capital District Boy Scouts, the light warden for the Albany area during World War II, the volunteer treasurer of the Albany

Episcopal Diocese, and the treasurer of St. Andrew's Episcopal Church. He also played the mandolin, loved baseball, and on occasion recited for me poems he had learned as a student. Like his brother, my father and my uncle, like myself and my cousin Julie and a distant nineteenth-century relative by the name of Joseph Haven, who once exchanged letters with Emily Dickinson, my grandfather was educated at Amherst College.

In short, my father was a formal man with a formal upbringing. He was a liberal democrat from a Republican lineage, married to a Rockefeller Republican. Politics meant almost nothing to him, relative to the larger concerns of the church and family, yet he openly disliked almost every sitting president. He had also met and corresponded with David Dellinger, the radical Christian pacifist, during and shortly after summer 1939, when my father was thirteen years old and Dellinger worked as his counselor at Camp Dudley, a few hours north of Albany on the New York side of Lake Champlain. Twenty-eight years after my father was last in touch with him, Dellinger emerged as the oldest member of the Chicago Seven during the 1968 Democratic National Convention.

My father had a swirl of contradictory influences behind him, as I suppose any man does. Yet he found himself a home in his vocation as few men do. He insisted on the dignity of his office and objected to being addressed as *Reverend* in the grocery store, at the barber shop, or at the Y.

As I look back on my own childhood, I sometimes think about Orwell's claim that the horrors of his British boarding school were exaggerated by his own diminutive perspective as a child—that those apparently horrific conditions were, in actuality, not quite so bad when seen from the perspective of the adult writer. At times, I feel precisely the opposite: Conditions in my friends' homes were actually worse than I imagined them, as I simply thought it a normal thing for eight members of Frank Johnson's family to share a railroad flat with six small rooms. There were so many families in Amsterdam living in such a similar way that I didn't give it too much thought. I didn't think much, either, about the spacious home we enjoyed, one block away from the Johnsons—four bedrooms (six if we count the third-floor apartment, seven bedrooms if we add the apartment above the garage), a large living and dining room, large kitchen, a screened-in sleeping porch on the second floor, front and back porches on the first. I think I was also not fully aware of the intense isolation my father and mother must have experienced as professionals—a priest and a sociology professor—in a Catholic, working-class town.

What exactly brought us to Amsterdam? Or more precisely, what exactly brought me to the point in my adolescent life where I was drunk and stoned late one night, in a basement apartment where we pissed out the door, and where, in the hysteria that only boredom engenders, a friend urged by old friends swung an ax at an old friend and I was one voice among many in the choir of that urging? How did my family move from the position of my great-great-grandfather, Erastus Otis Haven, second president of the University of Michigan, to where I watched Brooks in anger that one evening? There is still a hall named for E. O. Haven on the Michigan campus. How did we move from our connection with the Dickinson family to where I stood that high school Saturday? Joseph Haven taught at the town college when Emily was living in Amherst. The Havens and the Dickinsons intermarried. I still have my great-grandmother Kate Dickinson Haven's first edition of Emily's letters. How did I arrive at that Saturday night from the touchstone of the life of Bishop Gilbert Haven, a nineteenth-century Methodist abolitionist who had a book written about him and a cottage named for him on Martha's Vineyard?

I might try to pin it on my father, though I am sure that is not a responsible answer. Had my father never met David Dellinger, he may never have become ordained, may never have devoted himself to the social ministry. My father would tell me later that Dellinger was one of the most spiritual people he had ever known. He was, in my father's terms, a "self-giver." I know from my father that Dellinger had graduated from Yale a few years prior to that camp summer and had just the previous year spent weeks traveling the country by freight train with homeless men, sharing meals with them. The summer he met my father, Dellinger encouraged the boys under his charge to pray out loud together. Whatever spark of recognition occurred between them, in the day or during prayers at night, the thirteen-year-old and the seminarian formed a friendship neither of them soon forgot. Though my father was not yet in high school, Dellinger wrote him a long letter that fall and shared with him his opinion that my father should think seriously about going into the ministry.

Then, in the fall of 1940, Dellinger's picture appeared in the *New York Times* along with eight other students from the Union Theological Seminary in New York. Though as a seminarian Dellinger had an exemption from military service, if only he registered for the draft, he and the other eight seminarians decided to go to prison rather than cooperate in any way with the violence of war. My father, one year older by then, more fully under the influence of my grandfather, wrote to Dellinger at Union to try to convince him to change his mind. He never heard back.

At the age of eighteen, during the last year of the war, my father eventually went to Fort Schuyler to train to be an officer in the navy. The war was over by the time he graduated. Then he served the rest of his commission as an ensign in the merchant marines. When he left the service and prepared to apply to college, in the essay portion of the SAT he was asked to describe one of the more influential people in his life and wrote about Dellinger. Later, as Dellinger had done before him, my father would spend one Union Theological Seminary summer as an intern at the East Harlem Church.

One year after I graduated from college, in spring 1980, when I was living in Somerville, Massachusetts, and working for the consumer interest organization Mass. Fair Share, David Dellinger happened to call my apartment. My roommate, Alex Kuzma, a field manager in Mass. Fair Share's fund-raising operation, was also working as a community organizer in Dorchester. For some reason, Dellinger wanted to speak to Alex. I asked who was calling. When I realized who it was, I said, "Oh, you're David Dellinger. You once knew my father when he was a child."

"Of course I remember Robbie," he said, after asking me my father's name. Then he told me that he knew my father had published a book of poems, and that he owned a copy.

In Amsterdam, my father sought out the few black families in town and invited them to attend our church. They came. Mrs. Blood worked for us. Her grandson Jerome sometimes walked over to our house to play. Charlie Beekman was one of the best shots on our church basketball team.

Mike Teabout played on the team, too. Glen Taylor sang in the choir. We grieved with Mrs. Blood when her son Floyd, one of the town drunks, froze to death, passed out in a snowbank, lost in the end, as perhaps he always had been, in some indigenous white-out. There weren't many black families in town, but at least a few of them took to my father's church. Maybe penance for a childhood in a coat and tie, served by a black maid, was what brought us to Amsterdam from my father's Camillus parish. That is my view of it, my myth of him, my personal fable of how we arrived as a family in Amsterdam.

But that doesn't explain the ax. Once I had established myself as a tenured professor in a midwestern, regional university, my father in his own defense would often read to me a litany of all the local kids who became lawyers, doctors, one of them a judge, or who went to one private college or the other. My sister went to Vassar College, for two years anyway, and then to Trinity; my younger brother to Union College. I went to Amherst. Who can complain? We spent one month each summer in a cottage on Martha's Vineyard. That sounds to me, even from the inside, like a privileged childhood. But I still wouldn't wish on my son, my own daughter, the apathy of Brooks's apartment—the smell of our collective disregard for our own well-being as we drank and smoked, thrilled to some new puerile violation of the law, pissed out the door, and slept with girls we cared little about. That was the life I chose for the better part of three adolescent years, or to which I chose to bear intimate witness.

Of course, this is the story of a preacher's kid—PKs, as we call ourselves. PKs have an intimate understanding of one another, some secret knowledge of each other, into which no one outside the club can ever quite enter. The word on a PK is this: Either he conforms completely to the expected norms of behavior or he completely rebels. I add to this a third possibility—PKs sometimes swing wildly from one extreme to the other, conforming to expected norms of belief and behavior and simultaneously violating them. That is either a formula for anarchism or for wisdom, and in either case probably a recipe for disaster.

All the while I was riding with my friends in the cars we "borrowed," or was partying at Brooks's, I continued to serve as the head acolyte in my father's church. There were some very strange Saturday night/Sunday morning juxtapositions. One Saturday night, for example, we decided to go "bombing," as we often did in winter, throwing snowballs at cars from a field—a bluff that overlooked the high school hill. We would throw snowballs almost directly down at the cars descending the hill. But that night it was autumn. Someone came up with the idea of going bombing with apples. There must have been twenty of us. We might have killed someone if one or more of those apples had taken out a windshield. The apples thudded off the roofs and hoods of the cars. Some drivers, seeing the barrage coming, pulled over and waited at the top of the hill. Cars in the crossfire sped through.

Then we started running with the apples through the residential streets that led back up to Jay Vee's Pizza, our favorite warm-weather hangout on the hill. On the way back to Jay Vee's, in the frenzy of trying to get home free to the calm and quiet of mozzarella and tomato and pinball, someone started throwing apples at the windows of houses. Fathers and older brothers took to the streets. I started walking slowly, as if I had nothing to do with the mayhem. One of the fathers grabbed me. It turned out to be Mr. Gannon, the local jeweler and one of my father's parishioners. He asked me what I was doing there, where I was coming from. I was walking up to Jay Vee's from my girlfriend's house, I lied. He let me go. One of the more troubling moments of my childhood occurred in church the next morning when Mr. Gannon knelt at the communion railing to sip from the wine and water I mixed for my father. He was clearly shaken by the events of the previous evening, when a group of teenagers, for no reason he could ever imagine, smashed the picture window in his living room, maybe only because they were bored and it was asking to be smashed, or maybe because they didn't like the fact that he had a beautiful home. I never confessed to Mr. Gannon or to anyone my role in the events of that evening. My loyalties were with my friends, not with my father's parishioners, though I liked, maybe even loved them, too.

Throughout those adolescent years, as I smoked and sold pot and drank myself silly most Friday and Saturday nights, I continued to think of myself in terms of a Christian identity. Though I couldn't have articulated my thoughts very clearly then, in the years that have passed I have come to believe in Christianity as an indwelling principle. That is an old idea and certainly not original with me. It includes contradiction, maybe even insists on it, as one of the deepest qualities of a devotional life—as if belief, once it sets its root in you, is a permanent state of being and nothing you can willfully do can scare it from you.

Some Christians believe, without doubt, in the possibility of loving a complete stranger as fully as one does oneself. I am the sort of Christian who believes in that impossibility and continues nevertheless to uphold the value of an orientation to that ideal. We all fail our ideals and yet, if we are to avoid becoming cynics, continue to believe in them just the same: ". . . why abandon a belief / Merely because it ceases to be true. / Cling to it long enough, and not a doubt / It will turn true again." Or so Frost claims in "The Black Cottage," his words the voice of a minister who embraces an apparent contradiction—a commitment to two experiential truths: the unchanging realm of spirit, and the constant flux of the human and natural worlds.

There are truths layered within truths, in any human situation, and maybe the deepest truth resides in a tendency, an inward orientation, and not within the more superficial matters of conscious belief or overt behavior. Years later, living in New York City, stepping over bodies in the subway on one of the coldest days of the year, something that felt like guilt poked me in the gut. One man with a thin brown beard, wrapped in a blanket, kept calling out, as if he were still young enough to believe someone would hear, "I had the flu last week. I had the virus." Over and over again. It was either guilt or the impossibility of fulfilling the Christian ideal that haunted me all the way back to 106th and Central Park West. It was five degrees. At least a few of the thousands of New York City's homeless would freeze to death that night. I had an empty front hallway, an empty living room. At least ten people could have found warmth in the common space of my apartment. I don't think my first wife would have seen it that way. I too was not ready to put up with that sort of human trouble—ten strange people sharing my bathroom, maybe stealing from us, not to mention the stench. That night, not without some degree of guilt, I hoarded all of my apartment's eight hundred square feet for my wife and myself.

I often think of the lawyer in Melville's story "Bartleby," who at least makes an attempt to help one homeless scrivener. The lawyer attends Trinity Episcopal Church in New York City. Every time he attempts to help Bartleby there seems to be at least some ulterior motive—he thinks his charitable acts will improve his image among other attorneys, or that they will "purchase a sweet morsel" for his own soul's attempt to reach heaven. Melville seems to suggest the impossibility of a purely selfless act. Christ has set the bar so high that few, if any, human beings are capable of such devotion. Dostoyevsky's Ivan thinks so, too: The Grand Inquisitor imprisons Christ on His return. He arrests Christ for offering only despair to humankind in the form of such an impossible ideal of love and selflessness that all mankind can only hope to fail. I didn't see many people in the New York subway offering money, or their homes, to the blanketed poor bedding down, on that frigid night, on cement and cardboard only. Yet we live, nominally anyway, in a Christian culture. There were Christians stepping over those bodies on that night in New York City, and one of them was me.

I didn't think in these overt terms when I was still in high school, yet even as I slept with Maria Luisa I still believed in the ideal of Judy Tambasco, or in what she represented to me. I still desired nothing more than the undying love of one woman, and desired to love her in return, though of course I both wanted and didn't want to clip her angelic wings. I have asked my class many times, when teaching *The Great Gatsby,* what could possibly be the value of an unattainable ideal? That seems to me to be a crucial question, especially after World War II, for any Christian, maybe for all humanity—for anyone who believes in justice, love, or in the possibility of morality. Nick Carraway understood it: an inner commitment to a pure, maybe even a divine love, while the outer man seems to contradict everything the inner man believes. A fixed point outside the self, or so deeply embedded inside that we can never hope to hit it but aim toward it nevertheless our entire lives.

During my teenage years, I cared too much to avoid the usual fate of the PK: I rode in the back seat of a stolen car, smoked as much pot as anyone, and learned to box out under the boards with greater tenacity than guys taller and heavier than me, just to prove I belonged to Amsterdam,

New York. Meanwhile something waited and watched inside of me, something both compatible and incompatible with all the other selves I thought I had to be, as if, long before I had the power to choose, it fused itself to me—a presence I didn't simply accept or reject but knew enough to move toward when it moved toward me. It stayed with me whenever I avoided the rote smirk of adolescence inside a church—the children's choir singing "Go Tell It on the Mountain" behind the closed door they have just recessed through. It stayed with me in that sort of moment, after the Christmas Eve midnight service, when the adult choir joined in with the faint voices of the children, the church candlelit and otherwise dark, as if the only hymn in the world were distant, a whisper you hear only in the quietest moments. When I find myself deep inside a book, it is often the same sort of place.

12

Bass Line

But that still doesn't explain the ax. The last time I taught *The Great Gatsby* I was struck by what Nick Carraway says about himself in the opening page: "I am inclined to reserve all judgments, a habit that has opened up many curious natures to me and also made me the victim of not a few veteran bores. The abnormal mind is quick to detect and attach itself to this quality when it appears in a normal person." I mastered the art form, with regard to others, suspending all judgment, or nearly, also with regard to the "abnormal" behavior in myself. It has "opened up many curious natures to me." As long as I was in high school, I did not very often condemn Murph and Frank and Woody for whatever form of fun they embraced or found drifting their way. I do not condemn them now and try also not to indulge in self condemnation. Though I am slightly less forgiving of my own past, the ability to suspend judgment has helped me draw intimately near to a wide range of people, though sometimes at a price, sometimes smothering my ability to understand, in ever more complex ways, the human thing I am.

The suspension of judgment is, of course, one of the imperatives of the New Testament, at least as it pertains to the moral measure of other human beings. Like many of the wisest teachings, it is a double-edged sword. "All things have two handles," Emerson warns us in "The American Scholar," "beware of the wrong one." All the more problematic if things in our own time have twenty or thirty handles, at least half of them hot.

How, say, could I ever indict Murph, one of my closest friends, for grabbing a four-hundred-dollar electric bass out of a music store's display window and sprinting for home? Who knows what good came of that one audacious act? I didn't, even then, approve of it, as if it were for me to approve or disapprove, especially because Mr. Burton, the store owner, one of my father's parishioners, was a kind, generous man. Neither did

102

I do what might seem to be the moral thing—give my father Murph's name to pass on to Mr. Burton and the police. I stood back in a position familiar to me during my high school years. I was neutral, even passive, watching the course of events play out around me, while trying to maintain the veneer of my own poise amidst the surrounding swirl. That is, of course, the moral stance that good German citizens adopted on Kristallnacht, when Nazis in Germany and Austria openly attacked Jewish homes and closed down Jewish businesses.

Yet I wonder, in terms of Murph's amplified bass, under what conditions would I steal from someone wealthier than myself? Under *no* conditions? If I were starving? If my children and my wife were starving? I wonder too what good might have come of Murph's audacity, now that there is more than a thirty-year chain of events stemming from that one band of time when Murph utterly failed as a musician. Who knows if that bass guitar led him to Bobby Boyer, who, despite any personal loyalties to a friend, or because of them, told Murph, for his own sake and more fully for the group's, to give it up—forget the bass and, for that matter, any other string or percussive or wind instrument. *And for God's sake, don't try to sing.*

Maybe Boyer suggested, because he was his friend, that Murph try his hand at rigging the lights and sound equipment, and Murph went on from there to special effects, dry ice and smoke and that sort of thing, and it all landed him in Burlington, Vermont, where he found a good job and met his wife, and helped to raise his stepson, all the while drinking and smoking joints weekends and evenings. It didn't cost Mr. Burton that much—four hundred dollars, most of it covered by insurance—to make an involuntary contribution toward the raising of Murph's stepson, a human life he would never even know about. Who knows if that boy would have been better off had Murph never called him son—never entered the Vermont of his hurly-burly world? The moral possibilities are endless. Who was I to say that Murph or anyone, through an act of daring, should not try to embrace, in the only way he thought open to him, the electric presence of music in his life?

I am well aware of the extent to which that sort of thinking—the stance of the disinterested observer—veers down the long, black road of moral relativism. I also know that most moral absolutes—*Thou shall not steal*, for example—can't speak to the complexities of every human moment. The ability to suspend judgment tends toward moral apathy, on the one hand, and on the other offers the possibility that any destructive instance in human experience might reveal more fully, even if it takes thirty years, mitigating truths spawning within its wake. Whether such disinterestedness helps us live peacefully within the emotional turbulence of our own time—with the very real possibility that we are living at or near the end of history—remains an open question.

In some strange way, the suspension of judgment I learned during my years in Amsterdam provided me with a tool to navigate through the cynicism of an age that suggests, in ever more creative ways, the Orwellian truth that War Is Peace. Cynicism is an easy state of mind for anyone living in the decades following 1945. One does not need a Ph.D. to recognize the utter hypocrisy of an American defense policy—Mutually Assured Destruction—built on the idea of synchronized national suicide. Though I am not so brazen as to blame my own and my friends' adolescent wildness on post-World War II social and political conditions, I have read some accounts that attribute the rise in American alcoholism, divorce, murder, rape, larceny, drug addiction, violent assault, depression and other forms of mental illness, to the emotional and moral malaise of living for decades under the guillotine of American and Soviet nuclear arsenals.

The shadow of the omnipresent obliteration of everything human— the jitters of that pit and pendulum—might have shaken, so the argument goes, the central nervous system of anyone who was or was not listening. Why not go out and get laid? Why not wreak a little havoc? Get yours while the getting's good. No fun but in wildness, as O'Connor's Misfit might have said.

Or we might simply start to sing. We might whistle in the dark (as the bottles smash around us). We might hear *death* whispered in our species' collective ear—feel that one word seal itself in us, as if in the form of some new baptism. In the greater urgency of the modern moment, we might still believe *it matters only we are singing*. That is Whitman's answer to that one word, the hiss and lullaby he heard in the ancient mother of the sea. Though history keeps not ending, what would my generation sing toward the end of the last day, quietly at home or on some public stage? Maybe only through the suspension of judgment, somewhere in the deep, residual pool of our inclination, we might find, even in such a cracked moment, some voice to celebrate the limit of our lives.

My friends would have laughed out of the room anyone who came back to Amsterdam to suggest that Western technological prowess and the breakdown of stable forms—the church, the family, the farm, skilled and unskilled labor in relation to industry—had its grand anticlimax in the splitting of the atom, though minds more interesting than mine have said as much. They'd laugh if anyone suggested even an indirect connection between the breakdown of form and Brooks's explosion on the night of the ax. I'd laugh, too, then intently listen, then look hard in the eye and regard with great skepticism anyone who would offer such abstraction to explain the behavior of an actual teenage boy.

Maybe, too, my friends would laugh out of the room anyone who suggested that the decision by Mohawk Carpet Mills to abandon Amsterdam spiked those adolescent parties. By the time we were in high school, it had been some fifteen years since Mohawk Mills—otherwise known as Mohasco after a corporate merger in the 1950s—sold off most of its buildings and machinery and moved south, stranding in the process Mohawk Valley mill hands—some of them in the families of my friends—who had done no work other than to weave carpet for generations. Mohasco continued to manufacture carpet on a low-scale basis through the early 1970s, then completely shut down operations. Murph's father worked there for nearly forty years. He was given a two-week severance package and lost his pension.

"So what's your story, man?" my friends would have asked me, "What's *your* fucking story?!" had I dragged back from college to the bars in Amsterdam some technical academese to describe the shared tangle of our adolescent years. *"Whatever!"* I can hear at least some of them cry, along with the new generation, and I join in as we turn back to their jukebox, gin, blackjack, eight-ball, peppermint schnapps, and beer. Their two-down-and-one-to-go, fourth-and-long. Suspension of judgment. Maybe some good can come of it.

13

Skully Fags

All right, then, since no one really asked me, what *is* my story? Thoreau, in *Walden*, requires a simple account of every writer's life, though he doesn't himself exactly provide one, what with his omission of dinners at Emerson's and the fact that he built his house on the older master's land, the free use of which enabled him only falsely to claim his own independence in the form of a balanced personal economy. Thoreau recognizes repeatedly that he failed in his endeavor to live low and hard, but went "far enough to please [his] imagination," a claim that saves the beautiful veracity of *Walden*. A clean account of my own early life will also so thoroughly miss the mark that anything I say, to one degree or another, will float in my memory, and in the written record of it, differently than in the minds of people who knew me when I still lived in Amsterdam. The multiple, contradictory perspectives, the emotional range of my family, friends, and fellow townspeople, have their own different stories to tell, even as they may be the exact same stories I am telling.

I hope to go far enough "to please my imagination" and to hold to another standard: It may be possible to speak truthfully, even as it is humanly impossible to give fair quarter to the full range and complexity of each and every separate truth. I claim an attempt only for the former—only for an orientation to the truth, an attitudinal and maybe an emotional thing—even as the ability to render it fully lies beyond the realm of this one upstate New York homeboy. To what extent did I participate directly in the wildness that I have described in my friends? I will attempt here to define every moment during my high school years when I went beyond the pale, in serious violation of the law.

It began, for me, with an accident—a fender bender—that occurred outside the Amsterdam Y on a slow autumn afternoon, at the beginning of tenth grade, when Bruno Paglietta and I were riding, without his father's permission, in the Paglietta family car. The accident took place outside the gym, right across from my father's church. I don't remember whether I arrived at the gym in Pags's four-door, tan Chevy sedan, but I was with him when he backed out of the YMCA lot, the corner of his father's back fender barely grazing a young woman's car. Pags, too young to have a license, was quick to try to talk his way out of bringing the police into the situation.

"Hey, I am sorry I hit your car, but I'll tell you what I would like to do. I'd like to pay you cash for the damage. Would you take cash to fix the car?"

A fifteen-year-old boy was telling a young, grown woman what to do.

"Well, uh, sure, if I knew how much the damage was."

"Tell you what we'll do. You take the car and get an appraisal on the damage, take my license plate number. I'll give you my phone number. Call to let me know how much I owe you, but be sure to ask for me. Don't talk to my father, or my mother either."

The driver's door was slightly dented, the paint chipped away in a line at the creased center of a slight cavity, about the size of a fist. There was no damage to the Paglietta car.

"I don't know. Why don't we just call the police?"

"Well, then I won't be able to give you cash for the car. You call the police, my father finds out. Then we're dealing with insurance, your deductible, maybe his. I don't know what your policy is, and I don't know what my father's is. You'd have to get the car fixed. You can do what you want if I pay you cash. Keep the money, fix the car in a garage, find a friend to do it for you, save a couple bucks. It's simpler that way."

"I think I'd better call my boyfriend."

"Don't call your boyfriend!" The cars were blocking the side entrance to the Y lot. We weren't supposed to move or leave the vehicles after an accident. We knew that much. Paglietta's father was due home from work in less than an hour.

"Okay, I'll tell you what's really going on here. I've only had my license a couple of months. My father will kill me if he finds out I've been in an accident. Give me a break. I'll pay you in a week. If I don't pay you in a week, you've got my license plate and phone number." He was writing on a scrap of paper. "You've got my father's name."

The woman went for it, though it would have been better for me had she ratted Paglietta out to his father and the police. All the while this was going on, I didn't say much of anything. Pags seemed to know a lot more about cars and insurance policies than I did. I didn't really think the whole situation involved me. I was just trying to catch a ride home. But when Pags got back in the car, in his view I was sitting there right along with him, in the hot seat. I was in the car when the accident happened, so I was every bit as much involved as he was. I had to give him cash, or help him raise it, to pay the woman off. Pags asked me how much money I had in the bank. I had a couple hundred dollars saved from mowing lawns and shoveling walks but had no intention of giving it to him.

"Okay, then you're coming with me to go get some."

"Where are we going to get some?"

"I'll show you. Meet me tonight. Nine o'clock. In the woods on Major Lane."

The last I saw Paglietta, he was the only one in The Annex drinking straight club soda and lime, as if, in staying away from alcohol, he kept himself in a place above and apart from the rest of us. "Hello, Harc," was all he said, quietly to me, almost to himself, and said as little to anyone else, keeping to the end of the bar, near the door, watching us shoot pool and knock down some beers, then slipping out with the same old condescension, the same greater mass and height, as if he had somewhere important to go and wouldn't say where. He hadn't seen me in three or four years, ever since I left for college.

In Bruno Paglietta's ten-year friendship with me, the sarcastic, slightly mocking tone with which he usually spoke to me took its cue from his superior girth. Pags would later become a chef, an appropriate position for him given my one brief experience working with one in The Swiss Alps restaurant in Harvard Square. The chef there had a mild and sometimes not such a mild disdain for all waiters and waitresses, bartenders and maitre d's, for almost everyone except the owner of the place. Pags was destined to be one of two things: a chef or a lawyer. In the greater hierarchy of things, he deferred to no authority but his old man, one reason Pags and Murph got along so well, as they recognized and respected that trait in each other. The old man for Pags would eventually become the owner of a gourmet Italian restaurant, somewhere near Saratoga Springs.

I met Paglietta that sophomore night at the end of Major Lane, at the foot of the high school hill. He was carrying a bag with a hammer and a putty knife, and a couple of other tools. We walked up through the woods until we were directly across from the side door to the high school cafeteria. Even in midautumn, the door already had a temporary wooden storm foyer built around it in anticipation of the winter wind. The door to the foyer closed only with a latch; the inner door to the cafeteria was locked. No one could see us from the road or the parking lot once we were inside the foyer. The cafeteria door was an old wooden one, with eight separate panes of glass. Pags tapped at the knife with the hammer to chisel putty away from one pane of glass. Then he worked the edge of the knife along the side and under the pane and eased it out without breaking it. He reached his hand through where the glass had been and unlocked the door.

The high school seemed strange—a dark, vacuous place filled with the ghostly presence of known people and tinged with fear, the way a loved house can be when you come home to its emptiness again after long absences. That interior dark grew large, then larger, as we walked down the hall, even Pags diminished in the red glow of the high school's emergency lights. We found our way to two new televisions sets, mounted in empty, first-floor classrooms. I have no memory of where we hid those TVs, or how we moved them from the high school grounds, or what Pags did to find someone who would pay cash for them. Though I was still a chickenshit, in Paglietta's view, I carried one of those televisions out the high school cafeteria door. That was enough for him. He paid for the damaged car. I was temporarily off Pags's bad boy list, though I would soon be on it again.

I knew Paglietta mainly through school and, except to play occasional pick-up basketball games, didn't often hang around with him on weekends or in afternoons. He was only once or twice in my home, and I was only once or twice in his. But that sophomore year, when trouble found me, it was usually in Pags's company. When Pags heard that I had tried pot and was interested in buying some, he introduced me to Murph. That sophomore fall, if Pags was too involved with JV football to start fooling around with marijuana, he still knew exactly what was going on. I started hanging out with Murph and Woody and eventually Rod. It was with Murph, and through Pags's influence, that I committed my second crime, not counting all the times I broke the law by smoking pot or drinking underage.

Late that fall, Pags and Richard Podowski stole a checkbook from an unlocked car. They began writing checks to Michael P. Stankes. Dowski would write the checks out and Pags would take them into stores and endorse them. Or else they would work it the other way around. The trick was to have different handwriting on the front of the check than the fictitious Michael P. Stankes would actually flourish in person when he endorsed the back. This was the early 1970s. Small businesses in upstate New York sometimes cashed checks without asking for an ID. Murph and I wanted in on the action to raise some cash to buy pot.

We drove around one Sunday afternoon looking for someone gullible enough to cash a two-party check. Though I could venture a guess, I can't quite remember who drove the car that afternoon. My angel was looking over me as store after store turned us down. We tried a few shops in Schenectady and in Ballston Spa and then approached a drugstore in the East End of Amsterdam, where no one except Mary ever knew me. Murph walked in with me. There was an old man behind the counter. To prove my mettle, I did the talking. I told him how I was down from Troy, New York, visiting my aunt in Amsterdam. The check was given to me for some yard work I had done earlier that fall. I wondered if the old man would cash it to save me a trip back home.

The old man believed me. The check was for thirty-two dollars, written either in Dowski's or Paglietta's handwriting. I signed *Michael P. Stankes* on the back and took the money. On the way out Murph said, "Harc, you talk too much."

"It worked, didn't it?"

"Yeah, it worked, but you still talk too much." That was the first and last time I attempted to impersonate Michael P. Stankes.

Early that spring, when the snow had melted enough that we could shovel the blacktop courts off and play outdoor hoop again, with woolen sweaters and sweatshirts and the tips cut out of our gloves, I ran into Pags at Bobby Greco's house. Greco's driveway had a sharp incline. From the foul line you were shooting at a nine-foot basket, eight foot from the outside, ten foot in the lane. Pags wouldn't talk to me and didn't want me in the game, and wouldn't tell me why, except to say that I was a whiner and "a fucking goody two-shoes, and I want nothing to do with you." He refused to say anything more.

All this came out of the blue. I was puzzled for days until Dowski's name made headlines in the *Amsterdam Evening Recorder*. He and Pags had continued cashing checks for hundreds of dollars. Podowski was seventeen years old. Pags was not yet sixteen. Maybe his parents were better connected than Dowski's, or maybe it was his age, but his name never appeared in the paper. Still, he had to come in for a police interrogation. Dickie Hanes drove the car one day in February when Dowski cashed a check. The proprietor watched them pull away from his store and wrote down the license plate. Dickie, a good kid, never in any kind of trouble at all, found the police knocking on his family's front door. That led to Dowski. As Dowski later told me, the police knew about and for some reason didn't care to identify the owner of the third forged signature on the one isolated check. They cared about the second signature. Dowski gave them Pags, one of his oldest friends.

In all likelihood I will never know whether Bruno Paglietta identified me as the third accomplice in the forged checks scheme. I don't know whether Pags, through some skewed sense of loyalty, refused to talk when the police asked him about me. His loyalty wouldn't have been to me, personally, but rather to some tight-lipped image he had of himself. I don't know whether the police never asked about me at all, or whether his parents told him to answer whatever questions were asked of him and otherwise to keep his mouth shut. I wonder too whether Pags might have openly identified me, only to find that the police chose not to go after a small-town minister's son. Maybe one of my father's parishioners was already serving at that time as judge and refused to issue the warrant to arrest a member of his priest's family. Some time after I left for college, my brother was brought into court for riding his motorcycle in the road without a license. He came in alone, kept the whole matter hidden from my mother and father. Bernie Colucci, a long-time member of my father's church, was the magistrate or traffic judge by then. He dropped all charges and told my brother at the end of the hearing that he didn't see any reason why my father would have to find out. We played basketball with Bernie Colucci's sons. He had known us since I was three and my brother was not yet one.

For weeks I kept expecting a knock on the door. My nerves thrilled with every phone call. That nothing ever happened was one of the early, personal mysteries of my life. Paglietta's parents pulled him out of the public school and sent him to the Catholic Bishop Scully High. I hardly saw him anymore. I had heard Pags rag on the Scully fags many times before. Suddenly he was one of them.

That's about it, if we don't revisit riding in the aforementioned borrowed cars or driving my grandmother's Ford Maverick after dark, before I yet had a night license. Let's forget too the one minor matter of a scale stolen with Murph, slipped into a gym bag after school, out of one of the chemistry classrooms. The scale had a dial on it rather than free weights that slid back and forth, so we thought it was easier to use and more accurate. We could tell better, when we bought a quarter pound, whether we were getting ripped off. Otherwise it was just a matter of smoking and selling pot, strictly small-time stuff, drinking underage, a few experiments with hallucinogens, and driving under the influence. A fairly clean slate, relative to the local scale of things.

14

Reading

Until I smoked my first joint on the roof of the McNulty Elementary School, in the summer before the tenth grade, any signs of change brewing in or around me were largely internal. I still followed my usual routine: school, sports, reading. I had always been a big reader since my elementary days. That was another source of bonding with my father. I had to have a book to fill the yawn of any slow time—at breakfast, driving in a car, or during winter or rainy evenings at home, when my daily allotted hour of TV was up. I discovered one of my early reading passions over a bowl of cereal. K. C. Jones, the great Celtic point guard, was featured on the back of the box. I loved the way pain didn't often keep him out of a game, the way he played defense, swung the ball around, picked his teammates up, and didn't have to score a lot of points. That was the type of player I wanted to be. Soon, I read everything I could find on the Boston Celtics in the Bacon Elementary School library.

The myth of the Celtics, and probably the reality, was that it was all about the team. That our sixth grade basketball team went undefeated, 10–0 against all the other sixth grades in town, fueled my basketball frenzy. I started as a guard and scored a cool three points in the championship game. It wasn't long before Bill Russell replaced K. C. Jones as my primary idol, though I also read about Bill Sharman, Bob Cousy, Red Auerbach, Sam Jones, Tommy Heinsohn, Don Nelson, Satch Sanders, and John Havlicek. In the 1970s I continued to follow Boston: Paul Silas, Dave Cowens, Tiny Archibald, Cornbread Maxwell, Jo Jo White.

I later loved Russell as a sports commentator, in part because he disdained the usual banter of NBA TV analysts: He would make a perceptive comment or two and didn't mind broadcasting long stretches of silence. It probably cost him his job. I remember watching him on national television

113

when he walked off set in the middle of a playoff game in 1979. Russell was announcing the game with Rick Barry and Brent Musberger. At halftime, CBS cut to a photograph of Russell in high school, when he played for McClymonds High. Barry said something to the effect of, "Look at that big watermelon grin of yours." Silence. Musberger said, "I don't think you should have said that, Rick." Russell stood up and walked away without responding, leaving Musberger and Barry to explain, for the entire second half of the game, the televised void of Russell's monumental presence.

My fascination with Bill Russell continued beyond my undergraduate college years. In graduate school, I took an independent study class at the University of Iowa with a young Melville scholar, Jay Holstein, who was also a rabbi. I wrote a term paper on the inversion of biblical allusion in *Billy Budd,* essentially reiterating the position my professor took in a few of his published articles—that Melville lures readers into the text with the veneer of Christian symbolism, but is really playing a deeper game: Billy is not at all like Isaac, though the narrator claims he is, because Billy dies— ends up "fathoms deep"—while Isaac is gathered into the arms of the father of us all, Abraham. Billy is not like Christ, though his execution seems to parallel some of the Gospels' descriptions of the Crucifixion. Even John Claggart is not quite as demonic as he may seem, as he is referred to at least once as "The Man of Sorrows," a clear reference to Christ, and his initials are J. C. As Holstein would have it, Melville's text actually depicts a topsy-turvy world in which things are often not as they appear and often contain their opposites. Melville, according to my professor, actually offers a view of the world that challenges the stability of a Judeo-Christian order. There is no central spiritual hierarchy, in my professor's view of Melville, no God as chairman of the board, with the Bible as its charter. John Claggart appears to be demonic but is also something else. Billy appears to be an innocent but has the self-awareness, and perhaps the spiritual development, of a St. Bernard dog.

My education at the hand of Professor Holstein went on in and out of his office. We began to have bag lunches together. It turned out he was a basketball fan. Julius Irving's 76ers and Bird's Celtics were fighting, in those years, for the NBA Eastern title. Holstein was from Philadelphia. Though he rooted for the 76ers, he thought Bill Russell knew more about living than just about any man alive. He gave me *Go Up For Glory,* Russell's 1966 autobiography as told to William McSweeney. That one escaped me when I was a boy, or was censored by my school librarian at Bacon Elementary.

I was fascinated to find out about Russell's wild years. During one playoff series, when the Celtics were in New York, Russell drove, on a day between games, all the way back to Boston to see his girlfriend. They argued about one thing or another. She was a hothead. She would push him off her in the middle of making love simply because he seemed to be having too good a time. For one reason or another, in the middle of that playoff series with the Knicks, she stabbed him in the shoulder with a pair of scissors. Russell could barely lift his arm when he drove the five hours back to New York for the next game in the series. He and Auerbach collaborated on some excuse to feed the media. Russell played and won the next game—blocking shots, rebounding, tipping the ball to his teammates, and into the basket, all without the use of his one injured arm.

My interest in Russell deepened. I loved that he won so often, with less physical power than Chamberlain, also that he and Chamberlain were actually close friends and would sometimes share Thanksgiving dinner with each other's families, even as the media portrayed them to be nemeses. I loved that he refused to attend his induction to the Basketball Hall of Fame because of what he perceived to be corruption in that organization, and that he spoke openly about racism in Boston, something I knew about from working as a substitute teacher in Charlestown, Dorchester, and in the South End in the fall of 1979, just after the Boston bussing riots and prior to my departure for Iowa. The line I remember most from that book, and from my friendship with that rabbi of a Melville scholar, is Russell's quip, "Basketball is a game of leaping, and leaping is a universal expression of joy." Both my professor and Russell knew something about passion—that it pulled in about a thousand different directions at once. Joy was one form of it, and it didn't often come without risk.

My reading in junior high school progressed to real literature through Mr. Hanlin's ninth grade honors English class. That was the last year the Amsterdam Public Schools offered honors English. We read *As You Like It, Great Expectations, The Odyssey,* and *Animal Farm.* Though I didn't know it then, fat-assed Mr. Hanlin, who waddled rather than walked into class, was the last serious reader of literature I would encounter in my Amsterdam public education. In tenth grade English, we read song lyrics for our introduction to poetry and no real poetry, then simply started listening to songs. I remember bringing to class Jimi Hendrix's "Little Wing." The teacher actually liked it, but she stopped the stereo in the middle of "Purple Haze" and gave me a look. The class laughed.

Later, during my senior year in high school, once Frank had already moved out of Amsterdam, as much as boredom allowed me, I started a slow tack away from Brooks's basement. I stayed at home weekday nights to read and would hang out weekends with my girlfriend, and less occasionally with Murph and the boys. I read almost anything my father gave me: *The Jungle, Lord Jim, The Secret Sharer, The Nigger of the Narcissus, Heart of Darkness.* Because my father was reading Kurt Vonnegut, I read him too: *Player Piano, Welcome to the Monkey House, Cat's Cradle.* I am sure I didn't understand much of what I was reading but took at least something away from many of those books.

I have taught *Heart of Darkness* so many times that I have lost any hope of rediscovering what I first thought of it, alone in my room those high school evenings, on nights when I made a conscious effort to keep my distance from Brooks's basement apartment. But I remember feeling less alone in the world the one and only time I read *Steppenwolf.* I thought that maybe I could forgive myself some of my own weaknesses. It was the "Treatise on the Steppenwolf," a treatise on the self, handed to the main character prior to his entering the Magic Theater, that particularly spoke to me. It seemed like a gift, the idea that human beings were complex creatures, full of inconsistencies, that there were other people—maybe all people—who were less than happy with their own self-images. It seemed like a present Hesse was offering—that people needed patience and endurance to bring into one whole being the broken pieces of any identity, and that one might not ever really hope fully to arrive there.

Maybe it was *Narcissus and Goldmund*, the first Hesse novel I read, that sent me eventually to *Steppenwolf, Demian, Magister Ludi,* and *Siddhartha.* Thirty years removed from that winter's reading, I couldn't remember what it was in particular that so engaged my interest when I first gave myself to *Narcissus and Goldmund,* so I went back to take a look. I winced at some of the more unapologetically romantic phrases in the book: all the rhetoric about "the secret of his life," or his "hidden wound," or Goldmund's murky sense of some utterly individualistic, predestined path. As Goldmund heads out of his cloistered home, he bids farewell to Narcissus, his priest and only loved friend and the future abbot of the monastery. Through his newly discovered love of women, Goldmund starts down "the road to life, the way to the meaning of life." I cringed even more fully at Hesse's celebration of Goldmund's mother, who is variously portrayed in the figure of the Earth Mother, or of the Mother Eve, and wavers in and out of view in the faces of the many women Goldmund brings to orgasm.

All of Goldmund's adventures work to one purpose—to live more fully in the spirit of the carefree Mother. She "had known the same fate once. She had left house and home, husband and child, community and order, duty and honor, to go out into uncertainty." As a single father for more than four years, with the primary care of two young children, I was less than convinced.

What exactly was it that *Narcissus and Goldmund* offered me when I was a teenage boy, reading in my second-floor bedroom, my desk built into the wall, my father downstairs in his favorite armchair, my mother on the couch, both of them, after a glass of sherry or two or three, reading or watching the ten o'clock news? The idea that suffering might actually be a good and necessary neighbor, despite the fact that it didn't mow the lawn and trim the hedges, and let the garden go to seed? My guess is that the book spoke to me especially because the central figures involve a priest and a boy on the verge of discovering sex and violence and art. The priest Narcissus advises Goldmund that "the love of God is not always the same as the love of good." Maybe I wanted that level of wisdom and guidance from my father. I was becoming involved, during those years, with all sorts of people and situations and behavior to which, in my understanding, the church gave no quarter. Though my father never once spoke to me about adolescent sex or about fights with other teenagers, we talked often about literature. Hesse seemed to reconcile two apparently irreconcilable worlds. Maybe my father gave me the counsel I didn't know I needed in the form of Hesse's novels.

My older brother, though less of a reader and more openly in rebellion against the church, was every bit as much his father's son in terms of embracing contradiction, inviting it into his life, all in some sort of undefined spiritual pursuit. In college he returned to the violin as his primary love, and afterward shared with me an apartment in Boston, where he briefly studied at the New England Conservatory. He started playing for loose change in the Boston subway. Soon he tired of living on a pittance and amazed my entire family by apprenticing himself to a carpenter. It turned out he had good hands for more than the violin. Who could possibly have known? He never so much as lifted a hammer all the years he lived at home.

Within two years he was working as the head of his own construction crew. Then he took up boxing in the local gym. Though he was a heavy smoker, he'd work out two or three times per week and go three or four rounds with headgear, all the while keeping up the violin.

My brother would often complain that he was born in the wrong century—that 150 years ago no one would find it strange for a carpenter to play the violin and to know how to handle himself in a fight. Eventually he became a high school orchestral director and the concertmaster for the Southeast Ohio Regional Orchestra. He served for some years on the vestry of his local Episcopal church, where he still organizes and performs chamber concerts. I was moved in watching a recent film, Peter Weir's *Master and Commander*, to encounter in the main character a soldier and a leader whose passion finds expression in battle, and then more quietly, in a private hour, through a love of Mozart, one part violin, one cello.

15

Back in the West End

My friendship with Frank waxed and waned during those high school years. As long as we were out of the neighborhood, we looked after each other, as we had known each other longer than anyone else who partied with us in Brooks's basement. But even as early as the summer after our sophomore year, back in the West End our friendship began to show signs of strain. In August my family and I came back from a vacation on Martha's Vineyard and found a stolen ten-speed bicycle in the stairwell of our basement. Or rather, my younger brother Tom and I found it and hid it in the garage before my parents noticed. I wasn't too pleased to discover the bicycle on my parents' property, and was even less pleased when I found out that Frank had put it there. Frank hocked the bike in broad daylight, two blocks up Stewart Street, and had the audacity to stash it in my house.

That was also the summer that Frank and Bean partied in my home when we were away at Martha's Vineyard. Frank knew exactly how to get into my house without actually breaking anything. There was a small porch on the second floor, off my bedroom, with a door that didn't lock. Frank and Bean climbed up on the railing of the front porch, grabbed hold of the rain gutter, and pulled themselves up on the roof. They climbed onto the porch off my bedroom and came in through the door. Though Frank would never steal anything of substance from me or from my family, his sense of humor was getting reckless, especially once my friends got him going. Frank and Bean raided my father's liquor cabinet that summer. They sat around in our living room all afternoon one day, drinking sherry. Then they bragged about it for an entire week: "What *is* that rotgut that the Rev likes so much? How can he drink that sweet stuff?" They thought it was funny. I was less than amused.

Then there was a night in Tony's Tavern, earlier that post-sophomore summer, when for no good reason other than sheer boredom Frank punched unoffending Tony Marcello in the head. Marcello, the ineffective backup center on the high school basketball team, looked something like Mr. Marshall, Dennis the Menace's father. If Amsterdam was a football power, we always had lousy basketball teams. Frank dragged the straw house of six-foot-two Tony Marcello out of Tony's Tavern. He had to reach up as high as he could to smack him a couple of times in the face, twisting his punches as he had been taught in the gym by snapping his wrists when he connected. The whole thing was over in a matter of minutes. Marcello refused to fight. Marcello had done absolutely nothing to offend Frank, except for the fact that he was, in Frank's view, a wimp and a lousy athlete.

A few moments later, Frank sat back down to drink a beer with the rest of us in one of the booths. He was laughing and holding his head in his hands: "I feel fucking *rotten!*" Then he apologized. Tony Marcello was smart enough to take Frank's hand when he offered it to him or Frank might have hit him again.

If I was beginning to wonder about Frank's sense of humor, Frank's stepfather was beginning to wonder about me. Douglass Johnson didn't like my long hair. He held me at least partially responsible for Frank's shoulder-length shag. The early seventies was a tough time to be a parent. Despite the fact that he wasn't afraid to knock his kids around, Douglass Johnson was a decent man. He married a woman with three children and had three more by her, and supported all of them. Who heard of child support back then? He knew what was going on with Frank and Billy. If he was losing the battle to keep his stepsons from doing drugs, he intended to go down fighting.

One night when our junior year of high school held its breath and then exhaled into the cool air of June, Douglass threatened to call the police on Frank and me. My father had given my older brother Mark and me the third-floor apartment of our house for the summer if only he and I agreed to paint it. The night we occupied our first official pad, we did the only logical thing: We threw a party. Rod, Murph, and Woody, everyone except Frank in our main high school group, tiptoed up the apartment stairs, off the back porch of our house, sometime after 11 P.M. Chris Tambasco, my brother's friend from across the street, threw his nickel bag in. Since the apartment stairs could only be seen from the kitchen, all we had to do was wait for my parents to go to bed. It never once occurred to us that my parents, sleeping in a bedroom immediately beneath the living room of the third-floor apartment, might actually hear Neil Young's "Southern Man" or Duane Allman's "Mountain Jam," not to mention the squeak of too many Converse sneakers.

Before he fell asleep, my father came up in his pajamas to check on us. I cracked the door. He did not like that the apartment was locked—that he had to knock to enter his own home. He thought it sounded like a lot of people up there. Just Frank Johnson and Chris Tambasco, I lied. At the time, my father barely knew the Union Street kids, and Rod was from Pollack Hill, the far side of town.

"Well, keep it down and get to bed." My father made the mistake of trusting me implicitly, even when the evidence went the other way. Only a minister's kid could fully understand the mindset and emotional state of such a moment. I loved my father and loved too the illicit thrill of a party heating up. I went back up into the haze. We were rolling dozens of joints.

When Douglass Johnson heard that we had a sleep-over going on in an apartment separate from the rest of my parents' house, he vetoed Frank's request for an overnight. That didn't stop Frank. Frank waited for his parents to go to sleep, jumped off his second-floor back porch, and was with us before midnight, laughing at his sheer fool of a stepfather. Somewhere around 2 A.M. we heard another knock. I cracked the door and it cracked back at me. Douglass came bulldogging up the stairs, grabbed Frank by the hair with one hand, and pulled a bag of pot out of his pocket with the other. There was smoke everywhere. Frank all but fell down the third-floor staircase, with Douglass holding him up by the hair with one hand and slapping him down the stairs with the other, all the while hanging on to the pot.

A few minutes later, above the stereo, all the way up on the third-floor, I heard the one step it took my father to snap out of a deep sleep and get down to the back door. Douglass had called to give him a five-minute warning before the police came: My father was out on the back porch and up the stairs to the apartment before we knew what was happening, the veins in his neck popping.

"If there is *anything* in this apartment that you don't want me to know about, you had better get rid of it right *now*."

Murph slipped past my father and headed down the stairs toward the back porch, Rod and Woody right behind him. Then my father went down to wait for the police. We opened a third-floor window and started dumping bongs and water pipes, papers and one-hitters into the shrubs. My brother Mark and I ended up in our living room in a 3 A.M. heart-to-heart, our friends rummaging around in the bushes a few feet away from where we sat. They found the pipes and what was left of the pot, most of it mine, and smoked it all across the street on Chris Tambasco's front porch, where they could see, in the light of our first-floor windows, the entire span of our cross-examination.

The police never arrived. That would have made a splash in the local paper—the Episcopal minister's sons caught with bags of pot, not to mention the other things. Maybe it would have been my father's job. Mrs. Johnson saved our bacon. She laid the law down that night: No husband of *hers* would call the cops on *her* son and *ever* hope to park *his* boots under *her* bed again! Mary Johnson could call the shots in the family when she had reason.

The next day we led my parents out on a goose chase to the woods behind the Shuttleworth mansion, where we claimed we found two pot plants growing. We knew better than to narc on any one of our friends. We were grounded, permanently, for the rest of the summer, and condemned to paint the exterior of the house eight hours a day. By the end of the week the sentence was commuted to four hours per day on a ladder. Otherwise we were free to come and go. Still, we were relegated back to childhood and slept for the rest of the summer in our second-floor bedrooms, in our old twin beds.

It was a good ten days before I saw Frank again—as much trouble as he had ever been in, aside from that one day with Carla Tucci. I saw him from half a block away with a bucket of soapy water, scrubbing the porch and the stairs to his family's second-floor flat. Frank waved the sponge at me. I walked within earshot:

"Your parents let you out already!? I've never seen Douglass so mad! You would have thought I did something wrong, or something," Frank laughed. "How'd the Rev take it?"

"Not well, but at least Douglass didn't call the police."

"Yeah, well, he didn't have to hit me, either, the son of a bitch."

Mrs. Johnson caught sight of me from her second-floor window, in the front hallway, and stuck her head out, laughing as I tried to slip away: "I suppose you've known me long enough, *Stephen,* that you don't need to go slinking around the neighborhood. Are you trying to hide from me or something? You *know* you're always welcome in *this* house."

Six kids and Douglass to boot and she still had room for me.

Things were coming to a head that summer. Frank's older sister Barbara got married in July. She married Mike Furman. For years both Billy and Frank thought Mike was a fag and didn't hesitate to tell him so. Mike didn't often wash or cut his long black hair—a mass of split ends. Okay, he was a musician and all, had some mean riffs on the guitar, but they couldn't forgive that he never played a snap of football.

Billy had spent the previous year in Boston and then moved that spring to live in Georgia, near his real father and his father's relatives. He drove up from Atlanta for the wedding in a wreck of a car—a red 1963 Mustang convertible, with bald tires, a shot ignition, white vinyl seats, and a roof that leaked. The car turned over with a screw driver. There were no keys. Frank took to bombing around town in his brother's "new" convertible. He was as wild behind the wheel as he was in a bar. Frank didn't as much drive the car as he ran interference with the front end. He drove as he ran the ball, following the lead block, shooting the gap, and letting momentum carry him through any tight spots. The world beyond the windshield was not necessarily of primary interest when the party was anywhere else in the car. Sitting in the front seat with Frank behind the wheel was like the moment when you reach the top of a roller coaster. As gravity takes over you pick up speed, and just as you are beginning to have doubts you have no choice but to give yourself to the free fall.

Barbara was married in St. Luke's Church, a few blocks down from where the Johnsons lived on Division Street. The reception was at the

Holiday Inn. I didn't go but had the whole account from Frank: Everyone got shit-faced. I don't know whether Billy, having taken up again with his real father and his father's family, revisited old grievances, but something happened. Douglass swung at him and Billy decked Doug, tux and all, in front of all the guests, right there at the reception.

Some days after the wedding, Billy was arrested by the Amsterdam City Police for jacking up a Ford Mustang late at night in a used car lot. He was going for the tires. Though he was hit with a big fine he served no jail time. The town hadn't forgotten his contribution to the high school football program. In order to pay off the fine, he took a room at the Y and began working double shifts, 7 A.M. to 3 P.M. pumping gas at the BP station on Route 30, and 3:30 P.M. to midnight at Coleco Industries. A few months later, after paying off the fine and serving his probation, Billy found his way back to Atlanta.

All of this was just about enough for Mary Johnson. Late that summer, she moved the whole family to Indian Lake, seventy-five miles into the Adirondacks, an hour northwest of Glens Falls, where Douglass still worked. Mary didn't want the youngest Johnson boys to grow up through the same sorts of antics Frank and I and Billy were getting into. Frank was gone by the end of the summer. If he made it out of Amsterdam before me, he headed in the wrong direction, north to the sticks.

16

Kamikazes

I was wrong about my assumption when Mary broke up with me. I didn't have to wait till college. Christine Petrauskas was a majorette. I remember her panties dropping to my bedroom floor after a football game, late in the season, the first time she was alone with me. Then I lifted her skirt. She barely knew my name. She stood there naked from the waist down, all majorette from the waist up, including the silly hat. I was a senior in high school, she was a junior. She was a quiet girl, painfully shy—short, blonde, not as beautiful as Mary. That first day she only let me touch her with my hand and wouldn't touch me.

Then the prophylactic of winter set in. I still didn't have a night license. In New York, you could get a day license at the age of sixteen but had to wait until your eighteenth birthday to drive at night. Seventeen if you passed driver's education. Weekend days, my father would loan me the tight squeeze of his Toyota Corolla: bucket seats, stick shift in between, nowhere to go in the cold, what with the voyeur of the sun hanging over our heads. In warmer weather, in summer, depending on the girl, even in daylight hours there was the privacy of the river and the woods behind our school. In upstate New York's winter months, where was a teenage boy in the snow without a good set of tires and a full tank, and night's drawn blind through deep-wooded roads?

My Grandmother Haven provided a solution of sorts when she flew to Japan for a two-month visit, January and February 1975. My uncle worked for Dupont. His company sent him there for a year or two on business. He invited my grandmother to spend the winter with him. She gave me the keys to her Ford Maverick, just to keep the engine warm. I was supposed to turn it over every week or so. Drive it around for a few minutes. Friday and Saturday nights, I would walk the one block to her apartment on

Phillip Street. She lived on the second floor. Her landlord, a slight, suspicious man of about seventy, shared the first-floor flat with his wife. I could see him standing in the kitchen window every time I backed my grandmother's car out of his garage. He'd part the curtains and watch me until I was gone.

The landlord never said a word to my father but must have mentioned it to my grandmother. She never did to me, except to say that she found a girl's comb in the backseat of her car, and wasn't that strange? I loved my grandmother. She was kind and always welcomed the company of children—almost always said the positive thing. After she was long dead, I thought of her almost daily for a number of years. She was a major source of energy I tapped into as a single father. Still, the pulse of the moment during my senior year—the sheer possibility of pleasure—trumped any worry that my grandmother's landlord might rat on me. That Ford Maverick was the freedom to go to any movie in the Albany area, and the freedom to hang out at Christine's home four or five miles from the West End, where Christine's mother offered fresh-baked galumkies—stuffed cabbage—and other Lithuanian delicacies. It was the certainty of Christine's oasis of warmth in the deep chill of upstate New York. Only my grandmother's Maverick could truly access what we required of the dark.

It occurs to me now, only as I am writing this, that Murph and I, and Bean and Dowski all arrived at similar solutions to fill whatever void could only be filled through access to a car. We borrowed cars and brought them back again. Bean and Dowski perfected this approach when Bean and I were in the tenth grade. Behind Bean's house there was a used car lot. Dowski came up with the idea to slip the keys out of a car during the day. There were always multiple sets of keys in the lot office for customers to use when they took the cars for test drives. When the lot closed, Bean and Dowski would attach a stolen set of plates and fire up one of those babies for the night. They always filled the gas tanks back exactly to where they had been, and parked the cars back in the exact same spots. They got away with it for months, in fact never really got caught. Soon Pags joined the party. On a dare, I went with them for a couple of rides, Bean or Pags driving, Dowski sitting in the front seat. We'd pick up tacos and Cokes in a Jack-in-the-Box in Schenectady, fourteen miles east on Route 5. All the way

I'd fight to quiet my nerves in the back seat. I was with them, too, the night the police caught on, Pags behind the wheel, the cruiser with its lights out in the used car lot, waiting for us. We parked the car on a side street, stripped off the stolen plates, and scattered through the West End's maze of backyards.

Murph was even more reckless. He'd grab a car right off the street and figure he'd have it back again, sometime late that night, before the owner of the car, much less the police, knew what had happened. He took his chances. He didn't even bother picking up a different set of plates. All to visit his girlfriend in Watertown. My method was more cautious, maybe more insidious. I borrowed a car only from a family member, only from someone I knew would never press charges if I were caught. Murph didn't have that option, as his brother was the only family member who owned a car and his brother would have killed him. With less to lose, with no money in the family, Murph gave himself to the same act with more abandon.

The less chance my friends had for going to college or to some sort of trade school, the crazier many of them were during high school. I wanted both to break the rules and to remain in good standing under them—both to violate my grandmother's trust and to keep my place in her mind as a family member who truly loved her. Like Bean and Dowski and Murph, I largely got away with it, if I dismiss my grandmother's not-so-subtle comment about a girl's comb. Unlike Bean and Murph, Pags and Dowski, I didn't face the possibility of jail. On the one occasion a member of my family was arrested for possession of marijuana, my father wore his clerical collar to court. For the duration of the entire hearing in a Saratoga County courtroom, my father stared down the judge. Charges for possession and intent to sell were eventually dismissed. There was no police record. On similar charges, as a youthful offender, in possession of far less pot, Murph received the light sentence of twelve weekends in jail.

If I didn't have to risk my future in borrowing my grandmother's car, there was greater risk involved in what went on inside of it. I can only imagine now what would have happened to me if either Mary or Christine became pregnant with my baby. Lucky thing it took four or five times with Christine to get everything in sync. She wasn't one to complain and would probably have been just as glad—more than glad—to abstain. Once I had the logistics down, we practiced, like good Catholics, *coitus interruptus*, as if that prevented anything. I pretty much accepted Murph's down-home philosophy that "you had to get a good load in there to brew up anything." I can only imagine what Christine's laundry looked like—how she hid the stains on her clothes from her mother. My father had always been *laissez-faire* in his parenting style, except when it came to moral dilemma. Despite some occasional protests that I managed to talk my way through, he and my mother would largely look the other way when I stayed out to 3 A.M. But if I managed to get a girl pregnant there would have been hell to pay. The only relevant question would have been whether we had a Catholic or an Episcopal ceremony.

Mr. Petrauskas himself would have given birth if I ever fathered a child by Christine, as he wanted nothing to do with me and wouldn't recognize my presence in the room, even if there were no one else around. He reminded me of Brooks in some ways—quiet, sullen, watching you. Christine's brother-in-law was more loquacious in his dislike of me. I'll call him Joaz, Joe for short. He was a truck driver, about nineteen or twenty years old, with a wiry, muscular build. He explained that I had three strikes against me in the eyes of Christine's father. I had long hair, I wasn't Catholic, and most importantly I wasn't Lithuanian. No Petrauskas girl had ever married anyone other than a Lithuanian. Christine's older sister Linda had lucked out in finding him, in his opinion, as he was one of the few available Lithuanian men in Amsterdam.

The lack of Lithuanians in our hometown did nothing to temper Mr. Petrauskas's expectations. During the entire winter I spent in and out of his home, he only once acknowledged me. He surprised me one evening, some months after I had been dating Christine, by coming up to where I was sitting at the kitchen table, so quietly that I didn't hear him. He grabbed my hair into a ponytail and said, "We'll cut it off right here." Then he walked away. He had never previously spoken to me.

I made a point of saying hello to Mr. Petrauskas every time I came into Christine's home. "Hello, Mr. Petrauskas!" I'd say, and he'd look up at the ceiling or down at the floor, anywhere but at me. He wouldn't even take the trouble to leave the room—he'd sit down to read his paper, as if I hadn't spoken. This went on for the entire six months Christine and I dated. Joe was quick to assure me that, as far as he was concerned, the cards were still out on me, but he seemed to enjoy baiting an obvious specimen of a long-haired liberal, and a wiseass to boot. Joe was right about the wiseass part. Though, like Christine, I could sometimes be painfully shy, I had learned that subtle sarcastic remarks helped buffer my sensitivity. It was winter 1975, a few months before the fall of Saigon. I knew, he didn't, and I was going to tell him about it. For one reason or another, he had failed his military physical and otherwise wouldn't have been there talking to me, or so he claimed one night, over eggs and bacon in Christine's kitchen.

"I bet you never even had your face slapped," was his response to my question why he wasn't over in Vietnam shooting up communists if he hated them so much. "I betcha never even had your *fucking* face slapped." It actually took us awhile to arrive at this critical moment in the conversation. I can't remember what went wrong during his physical exam. The way he saw it, at least he tried to go. He knew about me and my type: I was going to hide behind the skirts of some chicken-ass college and let other people do the fighting.

He was right, or nearly right. I never would have considered going to Vietnam under any circumstance, and my father would have supported my decision. I had also only been slapped a few times. George Palmieri, a year younger than me, punched me in the face once, when my parents and I were out to dinner at Isabella's Restaurant. My parents had sent me out to buy a pack of cigarettes at a local store. There was no reason for Palmieri to hit me. He saw me in his neighborhood. I didn't belong there. He walked up and punched me hard in the face. I was shocked at how sharp his knuckles were. I saw him coming up the street but never imagined he was about to hit me. I must have been in the eighth grade, probably smaller than he was at the time. He told me to get my ass off his street. I did what I was told, one of the few times in my memory when I walked away from a fight without some face-saving remark that allowed me an easy out. I pretty much feared running in to George Palmieri for the next year or so, until puberty kicked in and I finally grew.

Of course there was the one earlier fight with Michael Leonetti, and the few punches Brooks got in when he jumped me on my paper route early in my eighth-grade year, though I don't really remember him connecting the way Palmieri did. I made it through one other fight in junior high school, and through my fight with Joe Camplone my junior year, without taking a shot to the head. I had only been smacked once in the face since I had grown to six feet, and that was by my mother, one early morning, 7 A.M. or so, when I was moved to play Leslie West's "Mississippi Queen," a raucus, heavy metal number, as loud as my ninety-nine dollar Radio Shack special of a stereo would go. My mother was sleeping. She didn't ask any questions, thumped into my room, slapped me hard in the face, and turned off the stereo. Otherwise I was almost a virgin in the face-slapping category. Christine's brother-in-law knew. But my girlfriend was sitting at the table.

"Why don't you go ahead and slap me in the face *right now!*"

"I think I will, you skinny-assed son of a bitch. I think I will!"

Christine pushed me out the door as her brother-in-law jumped up and knocked over his chair. That pretty much nixed my coming over for awhile, though we made amends a few weeks later, as people often do in upstate New York, during the long, slow, alcohol-fueled evening of a midwinter storm.

Upstate New Yorkers don't as much learn to drive *in* snow as *on* it. Even after the plows go through, there is usually packed snow all over the secondary roads. We learned early how to spin the wheel in the opposite direction from the car's fishtail, and to pretty much forget the brakes if the snow were slick enough. The trick was to drive so slowly that you didn't ever need to brake. You would certainly never slam the brakes on, which would send the car into a slide. Once a car went into a slide there was little you could do but try to steer out of it. I don't know how I managed it, but one evening during my senior year, with Christine in the car, I sank the back tire of my grandmother's Ford Maverick into a snowbank. We left the car where it was and walked to Christine's house. I was thinking all the way that I was in for it now, as we would need to have the car towed. My parents were sure to find out.

Christine's brother-in-law was all grins when he heard the news. He would have us out in a jiffy. His wife gave him a ride down to the yard where he kept his truck—a big flatbed. He had some chains in the cab. He hooked them to the frame of my grandmother's car and pulled it out. That was only the beginning of the evening. Someone had to follow him down to the truck yard so that he could put his rig away. He decided that should be me. On the way back to the Petrauskas home, from the truck depot, Joe insisted that we stop at every bar along the way. He was into drinking Kamikazes—vodka, triple sec, and lime juice—and insisted on the same for me. They were sweet. I only usually drank beer, never mixed drinks. These were hole-in-the-wall, neighborhood pubs, the type I had learned to avoid unless they were in the West End or on Union Street, where chances were I would know at least someone at the bar. Joe said these were his places, his people, not to worry about a thing. They looked like many of the other bars in Amsterdam. If you didn't live in the neighborhood, you didn't go there, at least not on a Saturday night. That was the night we became buddies: We had almost fought, we got shit-faced, and I owed him—he had helped me out. Now I was on his good guy list.

I bucked it up when I dropped him off sometime after one o'clock, then followed the sweep of the windshield wipers four or five miles home, the snow falling fast. I parked the car back in my grandmother's garage, walked the block to my parents' house, and tiptoed up the back stairs. The height of my friendship with Joe blossomed a couple of weeks later when we ended up at the Colony Mall on a double date. In the apex of our shared cultural life, Joe, his wife Linda, and Christine and I shared a bag of popcorn and watched *The Towering Inferno*.

Christine was about as popular with my family as I was with hers. I only remember her in my home a handful of times. Once, between tenants, we sneaked up to the third-floor apartment and made love in the front bedroom. Another time, my mother asked us to go to my grandmother's apartment to clean it in preparation for her return home from Japan. These were rare moments not to be wasted—indoors, alone together, with a warm bed and blankets. We made love on one of the twin beds in my grandmother's guest room, where I would sometimes sleep when I stayed with her. As far back as I could remember, my grandmother tucked me in when I visited her, first pulling back the same silky, green bedspread that we used that day to cover the bare mattress. When we were through, we used a soaked paper towel to dab at a wet spot. The wet spot bloomed.

Otherwise, Christine only saw my family when I played in church basketball games. Christine liked to come to all my games. It didn't matter to her whether I was playing for St. Ann's or for the Koller 49ers. We would swing out of our way to pick Christine up for the church games. My younger brother Tom played on the team. My older brother and sister were away at college. That meant Christine sat alone with my father in the stands.

"Who is that totem pole you go out with, Stephen?" my father would ask me after the game. I always appreciated Christine's quick whoop after each of my swished free throws at Koller games. But at the church games, she wouldn't make a sound. My father was an imposing figure—a big man. Christine, naturally quiet in any circumstance, even in the company of her friends, was moribund around him. Those games lasted an hour or more. He didn't see what I could possibly see in her. I wasn't sure myself.

17

Seder

On Maundy Thursday, the day after my dinner with Woody at Russo's Bar and Grill, I attended the 10 A.M. service at my father's old church. Mrs. Papura was there, Mr. Fallows, and Mr. Pettingill, who worked for a time at Coleco as a foreman. Tom and Rick Hayden's mother was there, too, and the Isburghs, and a handful of other familiar faces whose names I couldn't remember. I knew the priest was not popular among some of the remaining parishioners, as my parents were still in close contact with many of them. During Holy Communion, at the side altar, I knelt on the plush needlework of the communion cushions. The needlepoint was a series of images that conveyed the history of the Anglican Church in the Mohawk Valley. Though I was forty-six years old, the priest approached me on the communion rail and laid one hand on my head, as he might have blessed a child. "Ah," he said, "a priest's son, a *priest's* son," and only then placed a host on my tongue. He had a couple of boys himself. After the service, I learned who had graduated from what college, who was divorced, and who was dead. Mrs. Hayden kept telling me she never would have imagined that Rick, her oldest son, would have ended up in a divorce. She told me that she never would have imagined one for me either. I was married in that church. Many of the people attending that Maundy Thursday morning service attended my first wedding.

That evening there was an Easter seder in the St. Ann's parish hall. I agreed to come and kept thinking all day long of the needlepoint I had that morning knelt upon. My mother headed up the committee that designed the side altar cushions, choosing with the rest of the group an image for each period of the church's presence in the Mohawk Valley. The cushions ran along the front of the small altar and wrapped around one side. That evening I stood there again, among the stately presence of the dark mahogany pews, the touch of my mother's fingertips an arm's length away, spread out in soft, colorful rectangles. The first image was of the St. Ann Chapel, built square in the center of Fort Hunter, as if the church were the focal point of the first European military presence west of Schenectady. The date 1711 was stitched into one corner. A yellow plume of smoke rose from the chimney of one of the fort's four corner cabins. Three cattle grazed inside the primitive site, near the chapel. A wagonload of goods, pulled by two oxen, approached the open gate. Two Native Americans—Mohawks—peered above a slight decline in the landscape, watching the passing wagon.

Then I realized I wasn't alone. Mr. Engle, otherwise known as Bud—the church custodian, father of my church friend Tom Engle, and brother of my old soccer coach—had come in through the back vestibule of the main altar to replace some candles. He saw me looking at the cushions and came down the three marble steps into the chancel.

"I know your Mom worked on some of those cushions."

"Yeah, she did."

"They did a pretty good job with them."

"I think so, too. The second's my favorite, not that I like to see the church burn." Flames bloomed out the chapel windows like bright shocks of hair, the wild fringe of a bald man's head. The date "1776," in large red numbers, was centered above the burning building. Apple orchards and cornfields smoldered in the background, next to which the Queen Ann's Parsonage, a two-story stone structure, remained untouched, with a soldier, dressed in blue, standing in the door, apparently shouting to two of his men. In the bottom left-hand corner, three Indians were burying a silver chalice and a silver plate—a story I knew well. The original chapel had been a mission to the Iroquois. The praying Indians would later come to dig up that communion silver and carry it to Canada, where the Mohawk members of the parish had fled to avoid the American army. During my father's tenure as rector of St. Ann's, some two hundred years later, the American and Mohawk Canadian parishes were reunited in a "Twinning Ceremony." Beneath the three Native American figures were the words, "Last Mohawk Indian Village in Valley, Wolf Clan Castle, 1700–1775."

"Are you coming to the seder, Steve?"

"I'd like to, if there is room."

"Of course there's room. We'll be getting started in about ten minutes."

"I'll just be another minute or two. I'll be right in."

The next cushion in the sequence showed the date "1822," center bottom, in grey. Above the date, also in grey, were the words, "Original Empire Lock, Number 20." A cluster of men with wagons were carrying stone down from the half-razed chapel, another cluster fitting them into a half-walled ditch. The ditch ran parallel to the river, a double, asymmetrical S arching out to the horizon. The final cushion had the date "1888" in the cornerstone of the newly expanded St. Ann's Episcopal Church. Another cornerstone, in the oldest part of the church, was dated "1851." The church was center stage in the composition, with a single light in one of the upper windows. In the bottom right-hand corner, there were piles of rolled and half-unrolled carpet, in red and blue and black. A rainbow of buttons spilled out to the bottom left of the church, where there were also three brooms, the straw done in bright yellow thread. Behind the church, rolling hills, cornfields, and grazing cows, and two blue splashes, just right and left of top center, one with the words "The Mohawk," the other with a mule to one side, attached by rope to a boat, musicians on deck, and at the rudder a man yelling through a megaphone. The words "Packet Boat, Erie Canal," appeared in small letters beneath the image. A factory, the inverted exclamation of its round dark smoke and erect chimneys, filled each of the cushion's upper corners.

The side altar didn't quite make it into the twentieth century. Maybe they had planned a few more cushions for the modern era and never finished them.

At the seder, I was the youngest person by ten years. The new priest—new to me, though he had been there since my father retired fourteen years before—presided over the head table. He was a heavy man, with ruddy cheeks and a baby face, in his late fifties if he was a day. He instructed us to wash our hands in fingerbowls placed to the left of our silver. We ate a bitter sprig of parsley, touched with salt, and then said a prayer to remember the tears of exile and slavery. Then tart lettuce dipped into the sweetness of apple and cinnamon, four drained glasses of wine, and then, in whatever song we were singing, the unleavened bread traded the lead back and forth with the paschal lamb.

After dinner, two old parishioners told me how much they loved my mother as a pastor's wife. I had always thought she shunned a central role in the church. It was good to hear. The couple told me also how passive the new priest was—how he declined to do rounds at the hospitals, to visit shut-ins and the sick, as my father had always done, as if the pastoral ministry were no longer part of the calling. They said the new priest ran the parish from the seat of his office chair. The old cynical side of me wondered if this couple had said something similar when my father opposed the Vietnam War from the pulpit. I knew that the new priest was even more liberal in his politics than my father had been.

When I left the seder, I drove down to Guy Park Manor to take a walk along the river. It was dark, though I could see, some couple hundred yards away, the blinking light for Russo's Bar on the other side of West Main. The river was a black limb reaching off to some place beyond Schenectady. The current was strong, the water high from winter's runoff. I parked my car, stepped over the chains that marked the visitor's lot, and walked along the floodwall. The white stucco of the lockkeeper's tower shone in the moonlight like the helm of a ship, as if the river itself were adrift, buoyed by some immensity into which a human rudder dipped. Though it was April, the smell of dead fish and decay slid under and into the moist spring air.

I once felt that I was, or would be, an original mouthpiece for this valley, but suddenly I felt dwarfed by the longevity of it all. As the red and green lights at the top of the locks blinked on and off, I wondered if I had underestimated one of the most powerful presences in my life. In one fell swoop the Queen Ann's chapel brought the church and the military, God and his absence, interracial peace and genocide to camp along the banks of the river, and then razed the original stone edifice and placed its fallen walls piece by piece into the Erie Canal, as if to bless the one foundation fit for the valley's burgeoning commerce. But it was the river that brought first the chapel and then all these things.

Suddenly the tight yardless houses of mill workers stuck like barnacles on the side of the vessel of the river, as it drifted through and beyond me, age after age. Like some atavistic carp, scavenging the river's bottom, I had knelt, earlier that evening, in my father's church. It seemed a sort of beauty, the sheer length of it all, not a function of history, not a matter of miles. Before the first desecration of the North American garden, the Mohawk floated here, for hundreds of thousands of years. It would take an atom bomb to erase it from this valley. Maybe not even that would do it. Short of that sort of war, the Mohawk will survive us all, its tail in Buffalo, its mouth on Mars.

18

Five Easy Pieces

Frank came to visit me once at Amherst College. My father loaned him one of our family cars to pick me up for the summer. He arrived the Thursday after my last exam. We left the next morning. I loved the view of the college from inside the classroom, but my freshman year was a slow transition, never to be fully effected, into the ornate wealth and privilege of many of my classmates. One of the kids in my freshman dorm was driving a Porsche. I remember another classmate in particular, on the fourth floor of Stearns Hall: He had the annoying habit of asking every strange face in the dorm what college he attended, and even more astoundingly, how well he fared on the SAT. He had graduated from one of the better public high schools in the country, in Rochester, New York. Within weeks of his arrival at Amherst, he sported a new red beard and a cap, and began smoking a pipe. The world owed him a living. He was sure of it. He seemed constitutionally incapable of being anything but glad to see you, and felt bound by some new euphoric state of freedom to get shit-faced drunk on weekends, though he sure took care of business in the classroom. Even he knew better than to delve into Frank's academic record. I would have been running interference. Frank knew what the SAT was, and he knew a rich, snotty, upper-class son of a bitch when he saw one.

Frank and I went out that evening. I avoided bringing him to dinner at Valentine Hall, as I was afraid that some of my college friends might seem too dorky to Frank, or else too snooty, and wasn't too sure what the effect might be of either combination. I believe it was Mike Goclowski who joined us after dinner. Mike was a friend from an American Studies class who had a few carpentry skills and, despite his high school degree from Phillips Exeter, seemed to be aware of a world out there beyond Brave

138

Amherst. Goclowski and I were going to work together that summer, building a barn on his father's farm in New Hampshire.

If it was Goclowski who joined us that evening, he met us on the Amherst Commons after Frank and I had smoked a few joints and split a pizza. We were going to see *Five Easy Pieces* at the Amherst Cinema. I have always loved the scene, early in the film, when Jack Nicholson, caught with his oil-rig crew in bumper-to-bumper rush hour traffic, climbs up in disgust onto the back of a flatbed truck and begins to play a Chopin Fantasy on a rundown upright. He gets so swept up into the Chopin that he keeps on going and doesn't notice when the logjam of traffic finally breaks up, his car left behind, his best friend from the hard hat crew laughing with and at him as the accelerating flatbed veers off the highway into California's desert dusk. I knew right then, even as a nineteen-year-old freshman, there was something of that moment in my early life.

After the film, Frank thought that the guy didn't know how to live— that he worried too much about a bunch of old prigs on some island, all his family members sitting around playing ping pong and classical music all the time. They were holding him back. He had to get out and live his own life, in Frank's opinion, though he liked the part where Nicholson told the waitress to hold the chicken salad between her knees. Goclowski thought that Nicholson was running away from who he really was—that his family had given him a skill and he was afraid to accept it. He was afraid of success. I said I liked any man who could play Chopin and not give a damn what his work crew thought about it. I liked less the part at the end, when Nicholson leaves his father in senility, abandons his girl-friend, and begins to run again, this time to Alaska. We all agreed the girl on the island—Nicholson's sister-in-law—was better looking than his bleached-blonde girlfriend. Frank chimed in that anyone in his right mind would have fucked both of them, as Nicholson did, and Gock was gracious enough to laugh and did not disagree with him. We were sitting in a bar, then, on the far end of town, where the U. Mass kids hung out. I was making $8.12 per week, dishwashing four hours every Sunday in the Amherst College dining commons. I nursed the one beer I could afford. Then Frank said, "It's just a fucking movie, Harc!"

If Frank felt any discomfort over the twenty-four hours he spent with me at Amherst College, he expressed it only the next morning by throwing my grandfather's leather suitcase out of the Stearns Hall fourth-floor window. I had my grandfather's brown bag, a duffel bag, and a gym bag full of books, all set to go. My grandfather's initials, A. C. H. for Alfred Coles Haven, were engraved in gold in the thirty-year-old leather.

"Why carry the damn things all the way down the stairs? We'll just toss them out the window. The car's right there!"

I had time to say, "Whoa, Frank! Wait a minute, Frank! *Fraank!*" and they were already airborne.

Frank and I stuck our heads out together, from my fourth-floor dorm window, to survey the damage. My grandfather's suitcase was split open, my clothes spread-eagle all over the lawn facing the quad. The gym and duffel bags held, though I found out later the spines on some of the thicker paperbacks cracked. My roommate, Charles Stanley, a black kid from Philadelphia, smiled in wonder at Frank, kept smiling and shaking his head.

Charles was the sort of guy who drank tea. He walked around a lot in his slippers and bathrobe. He had all sorts of herbal teas and also regular orange pekoe. Occasionally he would drink one glass of wine. He would have a couple of his friends in from the hall and have a regular teatime. The day before, he was brewing up a batch and asked Frank and me if we would like some. I don't think Charles had ever encountered anyone in his life quite like Frank. He offered us the full range—Orange Blossom, Red Zinger, Aquatic Peach. Frank said that he himself had always only been a Lipton man. "I'm a Lipton man myself," I said, and Frank jumped up out of his chair and high-fived me: "Aaaalllll riiiighttt, Haaarc! I was getting just a little bit worried!"

We gathered the clothes up off the dorm lawn. The clasp on the suitcase was still locked, but the entire metal frame was virtually severed from the top of the bag. The leather on one side of the suitcase had also burst through, like a C-section that wouldn't heal.

"My grandfather's suitcase, Frank!"

"That old thing?"

"Yeah, that old thing! It belonged to my grandfather!"

"That cheap piece of shit? A little fall like that? It couldn't even take a little fall?"

"Most people don't throw suitcases out the window, Frank!"

"Don't worry about it, Harc, I'll get you another."

"Yeah, you'll get me another."

"I will! My mother's got a whole bunch of bags in her basement, up in Indian Lake. I'll pick you up one next time I go home."

"I don't want a whole bunch of bags. I want *that* one." I pointed to the bag.

"Well, right about *now*, I'd say you don't want *this* one anymore!" He kicked the bag then threw it in the trunk of my father's car, and we started the drive back to Amsterdam.

I was home for two weeks, until just after Memorial Day. On the Tuesday after the holiday, Goclowski was supposed to drive me to New Hampshire in an old red Camaro. His father had already finished the frame for a barn they were putting up next to their summer home. Mike and I were going to tack the sheathing on. But first there was the holiday weekend in Amsterdam. Word was that the party was at Northampton, an Adirondack campground on the Great Sacandaga Lake, thirty miles north of Amsterdam. I borrowed my parents' Volkswagen, threw a sleeping bag and swim trunks in the car, and called Frank.

Frank was scheduled to work that weekend, time and a half on Memorial Day, straight time on the other days. He worked as a dishwasher in one of the New York State Thruway restaurants. He was living at the Amsterdam YMCA. In winter, he kept eggs and milk out on the brick ledge of his one window. For breakfast, he'd crack a couple eggs in a glass of milk, swish it around with a fork, and swill it down. But it was spring and almost summer, and Frank was getting serious about putting some money together to get out of Amsterdam. He had left town for a year with his family, to finish high school in Indian Lake, and now he was back, needing to get out again. It wasn't much like Frank to miss a party, but he was scheduled to work. What could he say?

I waited until Sunday and drove up to Northampton alone. I was pretty sure I would run into at least some of the old crowd. The woman in the campground booth told me there were no campsites left for the night. I turned around and parked my parents' car just out of sight, one hundred yards down the road from the woman's booth. There was a fee to drive in for the day but it was free to come in by bicycle or by foot. To avoid questions, I left my sleeping bag in the car, figuring I could pick it up again after dark. I waved to the woman as I walked in. The lake was straight ahead, the picnic and bathing area to the left, the campgrounds to the right. I took a right. There were more than two hundred campsites, every one with a number, a stone fireplace, and a grill. I walked around until I saw someone I knew.

"Fucking Harc! Har*court!*"

"Murph, you sad-assed son of a bitch!" Murph and Brooks and Nappy and Czerew were manning a couple of coolers of Genesee Cream Ale. They had a car stereo going, both front doors open. Woody and Rod were somewhere around. I gave Nappy a couple of bucks for the beer and dug right in.

It was only later that evening, when the sun was starting to set, that I realized I had made a fatal mistake in leaving my sleeping bag in my parents' car. There were all sorts of kids still in high school in the campsites around us. Everyone seemed to be pairing up for the night. Earlier Woody connected with some big-boned, good-looking girl. They took off for a couple of hours. She was a year or two behind us in school. Her boyfriend, not a small guy, kept showing up looking for Woody. Then Woody finally came back and called the boyfriend by his name, almost in a friendly way, and told him, "Go get lost now. I don't want to hit you. Don't make me hit you." The boyfriend swung at Woody. Woody knocked his glasses off. Then he knocked him down. The boyfriend did the smart thing and got up and walked away.

That evening, I found myself in the company of Sharon Sabato, a petite, pretty Italian girl who must have been a junior in high school. I wasn't worried about her age, or the fact that my younger brother once had an elementary school crush on her. Rumor had it that Paddy Lucas was also after her. That should have concerned me, too, but didn't. I would be gone in two days and Sharon was snuggling up to me by the fire. I was open to possibility and Sharon was a possibility open to me. I had run into her once before, at night in the baseball diamond dugouts on the high school fields, where we drank and smoked pot, the escape of the woods nearby in case the police came by on rounds. We sat with the others in a semicircle around the fire. Murph had taken up with Sue, a girl I briefly dated in high school.

What kept me from going with the drift of the moment was that it was May in the Adirondacks. All I had on was a jean jacket. I didn't know what the sleeping arrangements were going to be, whether the Sabato girl was inviting me into her tent or whether she and her friends would insist on throwing me out. It would hit forty degrees that night, or close. I told the Sabato girl I had to get my sleeping bag from the car and would be right back. There were a few minor problems with my modus operandi, not to mention the major ones. I had no flashlight and the park was quickly going dark. The serpentine maze of campsites wound through the woods. The lake slipped in and out and around them. I had also drunk about all I could handle, which meant I had sucked down ten to twelve Genesee Cream Ales. On the way out to the car, I saw a flashlight coming at me: a New York State park ranger asked to see my site permit. I always prided myself, during my Amsterdam years, in my ability to sober up in the heat of the moment.

"I left it back at the campsite, officer."

"Do you know your site number?"

"Nope."

"Let's see some ID." I fished out my driver's license. "Are you registered with the park?"

"What exactly do you mean by registered?"

"Every site number has a limit of six campers. Each camper's name is registered with a site. Do I need to call my office?"

"Well, officer, I was just kind of visiting some friends here. I am just back from college."

"Well, I will give you a warning this time."

He walked me to the front gate of the park. I went out to the trunk of my parents' car, grabbed my sleeping bag, and headed right back in. By then it was night in earnest. The only lights in the entire campgrounds were near the public bathrooms. I turned in the direction of the campsites, as I had earlier in the day. I could feel the road beneath my feet but couldn't tell where it was going. Every time it curved I found myself in leaves, tripping over a tree stump or sticks, and shuffled my way back to blacktop.

Now and then a kerosene lantern or a campfire carved a site number in an arc of light. I had my sleeping bag under my arm. After a half an hour or more, I thought I might have to pick a random spot on the roadside and sleep until sunrise, with the thought of Sharon Sabato just beyond reach in the dark. At that point I began to hope for anyone who could lead me out or further into the campground. I saw the firefly of a flashlight in the distance, far up the black gulf of the road, and made my way toward it. The light jerked down, then up, then back and forth, as if purely random in its movements, like a fluorescent ball against the walls and floor of an entirely dark squash court. As I drew closer, I could see a group of people gathered around the man with the light.

"Hey, you wouldn't happen to know Joe Murphy or Mike Weil, or at least the way back to the gate?"

He knew who I was the instant the beam flashed in my face. I saw his broad-rimmed hat and began to run toward what seemed to be an opening in the woods, from what I could make out from the tops of the trees silhouetted against the sky. He was right behind me, with the advantage of the light. I sprinted up the road. Something like quicksand, but colder, made an open field tackle, cutting my feet out from under me. I hit the lake running, went down with my sleeping bag, the park ranger watching, waiting on the beach, shining the flashlight in my face.

"Now aren't you ashamed of yourself, all soaking wet like that."

I sat in the water for a few stunned seconds. There was nowhere to go but out. The ranger kept me at arm's length as he dragged me by my shirt back up the access road. He wrote me out a summons to appear in court, in Northville, on June 24, 5 P.M., then walked me out to the gate. My sleeping bag had tripled in weight. Before he let me go, he offered personally to drive me to the county jail if he found me in the park again that night. I went out to my parents' car and changed under cover of dark into my swimsuit—a pair of cutoff jeans. I had no shirt. I dried off with a towel then wrapped it around my shoulders and pulled out of the park, my bare foot on the gas. When I hit Route 30, I sat at the intersection for a full minute or more. As long as I kept the engine running, I would be warm. I had about a quarter tank of gas, with no chance that any gas station would be open until morning. I could drive thirty miles home and call it a night or look for other parties in other campgrounds. There had to be another Sharon Sabato out there! I took a right, rather than a left toward Amsterdam, and drove the fifteen miles north to Wells and Lake Algonquin.

There was a big bonfire burning when I crossed the bridge from Route 30 to where smaller dots of light were strung out in a straight line along the lake. I knew the campground well, as my older brother and I had spent time together there, hitchhiking up from Amsterdam. The Wells sites were free, the campground much smaller than the one in Northampton. There was no front gate, no woman in a booth, no registration that I knew about. The shadows of seven or eight people were gathered around the big fire. One of them approached me when I pulled up:

"Fucking Harcourt! It's fucking Harc!" Jeff Van Epps, one of the Union Street kids a year older than Murph and me, emerged Jack-o-lantern-like from the glare of the bonfire and the dark. In my headlights, illuminated from below, his face seemed to bend rather than lean toward the car. Jeff was a happy drunk. Then he looked in the back seat to see who was with me.

"Fucking Hark the Herald Angels Sing! What are you doing up here?" I stepped out of the car, barefoot, the towel pulled tight around my neck and shoulders.

"Get a load of the cape! What are you, Clark Kent? Get some clothes on, man! What are you, crazy!?"

I knew the answer to that one: "Crazy enough to drink a beer!"

I didn't know anyone else there except Jeff's girlfriend. She made enough money in her job as an operator with the telephone company to keep them both in gas and beer. Jeff seemed constitutionally opposed to work. He would make novelty arts and crafts items and sell them at craft shows. Anything that would bring a buck in without actually having to work a nine-to-five. Otherwise, he had found the good life. He had an old lady who would take care of him.

"Anybody want to go for a swim? Harc's going for a swim! It's fucking forty degrees!" Jeff was laughing more with than at me, and wanted to hear the whole story. I dragged a picnic table as close to the fire as I dared, pulled my towel around my shoulders, and babied my beer. No one offered me a spare shirt or sweatshirt or pair of pants, and I wasn't asking. Soon everyone started drifting off to wherever they had staked their tents for the night. I spent the rest of the night alone, feeding the fire, chilled to the bone. I started the car up, for ten or fifteen minutes every hour or so, until the gauge pointed to the red bar on the wrong side of empty. By morning, the entire front of my body was burned from sitting too close to the fire. I waited until I thought some gas stations would be opening up and took off sometime after 8 A.M., everyone else still sleeping.

When I got home, I threw my wet clothes and sleeping bag in the wash. "What did you do, spend the entire day lying on your back?" my mother asked me when I came into the kitchen, still in my cutoffs, the back half of my body a luminescent white, the front half bright red.

Mike Goclowski came by the next day in his red Camaro. My father helped us rig a couple of suitcases on top of his luggage rack. I thought I would be gone without returning for the entire summer, but now I had a June 24th date, thirty miles north of Amsterdam. Goclowski and I had an easy enough job for the first weeks of June, cutting up old barn board with a circular saw and nailing whatever odd pieces would fit into the frame his father had already raised. The Goclowski farm was a few miles south of Littleton, near where I had worked the previous summer, in Bethlehem, New Hampshire. As the end of June approached, Goclowski's parents decided to take him to Europe for the rest of the summer. I hitchhiked into Bethlehem, lined up a job for the months of July and August at the Perry House Hotel, then headed back to upstate New York to appear in court.

Somewhere in southern Vermont, on Route 4, on the way back to Amsterdam, I was picked up by a Mack truck driver, the first and only time I was ever propositioned while hitchhiking. The truck driver claimed to be lost and asked me if I knew the fastest way to get to Albany. I told him to stay on Route 4 until he hit the Northway, then to turn south. He had some pornographic magazines beneath his seat and tossed one on my lap.

"Want to look at that?"

"Not really."

"How about this one?"

He flipped to a centerfold, guys and girls all going at it, all parts greased and interactive.

"Does that do anything for you?"

"No, not really."

"How about one of these, then?"

The centerfold showed two men giving oral sex to one another.

"Definitely not."

"You ever think about getting it on with a guy?"

"Nope."

"Why not?"

"I get into enough trouble with women."

"Well, it might be worth some money to you. You want to make some money?"

"I don't think so."

An unnatural silence set in. I was glad he was driving a Mack truck, rather than a car or pickup, as he couldn't easily turn off unnoticed onto some small dirt road. When we hit the Northway he pulled into the breakdown lane.

"Look, it's nothing personal, but get the fuck out of the truck."

"What?"

"I said get out of the truck."

I climbed the two steps down off the cab of the truck and stood in the wake of my lost ride to Albany, my heart pumping.

When I finally made it back to Amsterdam, I borrowed fifty dollars from Frank in case the court fine was more than I imagined. There were about twenty of us gathered in the judge's living room, right there on Main Street, in Northville. The park ranger who had been on duty that night called us into the judge's bedroom one by one. We could either pay a twenty-seven dollar fine to forget the whole thing or set up a date to appear in county court. I paid the fine and did the math: Between them, the ranger and the judge made over five hundred dollars that night.

19

Marina and Ray Green

The rest of my summer was spent at the Perry House, in Bethlehem, New Hampshire. All of the guests were Orthodox Jews, the waiters, bellhops, and waitresses mainly Jewish kids from New York City who did not care one way or the other about kosher food. The town was known especially for its Hasidic Jewish hotels, though there was also the Orthodox Perry House, a B'hai center, and a Hindu Premi House nearby, complete with a restaurant and bakery run by the followers of Guru Maharaji. At night, with almost no streetlights in town, in the deep dark, Hasidic chants wound in and above the pulse of cicadas. Many of the hotels in Bethlehem were founded in the age before air conditioning, when Orthodox and Hasidic Jews would come up from New York City for relief from the allergy season. Now they came for the food and the cool mountain air, the Ammonoosuc River nearby, Franconia Notch right down the road.

In the last days of June, I worked doing odd jobs to help set the hotel up for the summer—painting the pool, varnishing the dining room floor— and then in July wore a yarmulke and worked inside as a bellhop and busboy. It was there, at the Perry House, that I met Marina. I thought, at the time, that she was the first real love of my life. She was one of the waitresses, a painter from New York City, twenty-three years old and already a Cooper Union graduate. During the year I spent with Marina, I saw Nureyev dance with the New York City Ballet, traveled during Christmas vacation through the Yucatan to Pelenque and San Cristobal de las Casas, and thumbed back and forth for the rest of the academic year, from Amherst to her family's summer cottage in Woodstock, and to her Manhattan apartment. I also began to play the cello again, this time in earnest. It was quite a stretch, that summer, from the sixteen-year-old arms

148

of Sharon Sabato to the twenty-three-year-old painter Marina Epstein and everything she had to show me.

Ours was a summer romance that seemed to end badly when Mrs. Perry fired me toward the end of the season. The baker, an older black guy from Harlem, had either quit or been let go. Marina and I moved into the larger apartment he vacated, in the dormitory where the rest of the help had single rooms. This arrangement either offended Mrs. Perry's sensibilities, or she was trying, late in the summer, to stay open through Labor Day with a scaled-back staff. What she didn't count on was that Marina would quit, too. Marina called me a few days after I left to say that she was going to follow me back to Amsterdam. By then I was in Indian Lake, visiting the Johnson home.

Looking back, that was the summer I began a measured swing, though I didn't know it then, from the tonic of Amsterdam to the dominant of what I thought Marina represented—music and art, ballet, travel through foreign countries, literature, and sex that involved at least a degree of love with a beautiful woman. I thought I might steer by her North Star. Yet according to the basic rules of music theory, the tonic leans toward the instability of the dominant, only to resolve finally on its home note again. I knew enough never to introduce Marina to Frank, Murph, and Woody, though eight years later I brought Yong Soon, a Korean painter I met at Yaddo, to Woody's and Gina's trailer. We were driving a Honda. Woody, forever a union man, came out of the front door shouting, "Hey, HarCOURT! Get that Japanese piece of shit off my lawn!" Woody was joking. He was referring to the car. Yong Soon wasn't so sure.

When I finished that summer in New Hampshire, new worlds seemed to be opening, but old loyalties kept pulling me back to the Johnsons. When I found my way to Indian Lake, after hitchhiking across Vermont and up the New York Northway, Frank's mother, Mary Johnson, answered the door. Frank was a couple miles down Route 30, doing some yard work for an older woman. Mrs. Johnson told me where I could find him. The Johnson house was a large, cabinlike structure, with an open, loftlike attic, partially finished with a new particle board floor. All the Johnson boys slept there. There were fresh rolls of insulation tacked in the open bays of the rafters. I gave Mrs. Johnson the gifts I brought, a loaf of fresh baked bread and a couple pounds of granola, left my bag upstairs, and went out to find Frank.

I caught a ride down Route 30 to where Frank was raking up cut grass. He was about to enlist in the navy. He moved back home for a few months before heading out for boot camp. Billy, already an army ranger, was home on leave. Mary Caprara, a former cheerleader and the best violinist during my years in Amsterdam's Wilbur H. Lynch High School, was up visiting Billy. They would eventually marry. We went out that night drinking with the younger, local crowd, which in Indian Lake meant anyone from age fourteen to twenty-five. There was one bar in the town center and one A&P grocery store.

The next morning Billy and Douglass, Frank and the quieter, younger Mary, played Greek chorus to the older Mary's lead:

"Stephen, we love that homemade bread you bought for us, but don't be bringing any horse food into this house. Billy, are there any horses around here that you know about? Any horses we can feed this stuff to?"

She was holding up the bag of granola for everyone to see, everyone at the table, Frank, Billy, Douglass, Mary Caprara, the younger boys Matt and Gary, the whole family laughing, including me.

"You really eat that horse food, Stephen?"

"Sure! I think I'm good for a bowl right about now!"

The bag of granola came home with me when I hitchhiked the seventy-five miles south to Amsterdam and waited for Marina to join me.

That was the last I saw of Frank, for almost nine years, until I stopped by his navy base in Charlotte, South Carolina, in 1985. Then I saw him one other time when he drove up to Amsterdam for my first wedding, in 1989. That was about it, though for years, whenever I made a move—rented a new apartment, started a new job—I would dream about Frank or Billy, or Mary Johnson. I would be lying in the arms of a woman I had only recently begun to love, and there Frank would be again, hovering on the edge of some new consciousness early in the morning. Even in Beijing, on one of my first weeks there, after jetlag had worn away, I woke in my mother-in-law's apartment at sunrise with dozens of elderly men and women doing Tai Chi in the yard. Trying, quite literally, to *orient* myself, I remember saying, inwardly, that whatever God might be, he was here, in this strange country, as much as anywhere, and realized only then I had thought once more in my sleep of my oldest friend.

Marina and I drove to Miami that next Christmas and flew for $110 roundtrip from Florida to Cancun, the first time I had ever been on a plane. We spent two nights on Isle Mujeres and traveled by bus to Chichen Itza and Merida, and then by train to Pelenque and San Cristobal. We lived mainly on fruit we could peel—bananas and oranges—and on bottled water. Tourista set in only in the last few days of the trip, when we had already circled back to Cancun. We spent a total of $400 each on the entire adventure. On the drive home to Edgewater, New Jersey, where Marina's parents lived, we put all the money we had left into three tanks of gas and tolls and drove nonstop, our stomachs too queasy to worry much about food. We were gone a little more than a month. I was almost twenty.

We didn't actually split up until the following August, but by March I was making what my father thought were considered decisions in staying on campus weekends to study, rather than catching a ride or hitch-hiking to see Marina in the city. Marina found this new studiousness to be evidence of the lack of any real passion in my life. My grades had slipped considerably the previous semester. I was in the process of bringing them back up. What she desired from me was what she thought I lacked—a willingness to live fully in the moment. I was too careful, in her view—a typical American. I was thinking of law school—an insurance policy against fate, in her opinion. I was too willful, trying to control the future, when for all I knew I might be dead in a year. I had already eaten my cake, in Marina's opinion, and wanted it freeze-dried, too.

Marina would make, each summer, enough money as a waitress to live frugally for the rest of the year. She cared about her painting, not about her career. She actually believed the spirits of dead artists were alive and communing with her on a daily basis. When she told me *that* one, I asked her to have them give me a phone call, too. When I visited her at her parents' home, her father didn't care if we slept in the same bed. When she came to my home, my parents sequestered her in the far bedroom and watched the door. My grandmother would barely speak to her.

My decision to focus on my courses extended, that sophomore year, through to the end of finals. Gradewise, that was my strongest semester at Amherst College. I was taking mainly history and literature classes. But I had been so preoccupied on campus that I had no work lined up for the summer. Marina headed to the Catskill Mountains to work at another Jewish resort. I went home for the last stretch of time I would spend living in Amsterdam.

"Just because you can't find a job doesn't mean you can get so grouchy with everybody else at home, Stephen," my father warned me after my first few weeks back from my sophomore year. I had pumped gas one earlier summer on the New York State Thruway but left a few weeks before the season ended. The manager remembered and wouldn't take me back again. I finally found a job for minimum wage at the BP station on Route 30, going north out of Amsterdam. I worked there for a few weeks until some money was stolen during one of the evening shifts. The BP shift manager, cashing out at the end of the day, had left his bill roll on the desk when he went to use the bathroom. It was gone when he came back. Everyone on the shift was forced to empty his pockets. No one had more than the usual hundred dollars or so we were allowed to carry. The entire shift was laid off.

It turned out that a kid named Paul had taken the money. He hid it in his car, behind the station, then panicked over the next few days when the owner of the gas station brought in Bureau of Criminal Investigation state police to interview anyone who was working that night. Paul called me three or four days after the robbery and told me he had heard a rumor that I had stolen the money. He said he knew I didn't do it and that we had better stick together. Then he had his girlfriend make an anonymous call to the BCI investigators. She offered to return the money to the girls' bathroom at Carol's Hamburgers, right down the road from the BP station. They promised her that no charges would be filed as long as they received all the money back. The BCI investigators staked out the girls' bathroom at Carol's Hamburgers and arrested Paul's girlfriend when she showed up to return the money. She informed on her boyfriend. Once they picked him up, everyone else on the shift was hired back again.

By then I was already working at Coleco Industries, where I was making more than the minimum wage BP paid—$3.12 per hour, time and a half on weekends. Mr. Pettingill, a vestry member in my father's church and a foreman at Coleco, helped me get a job working for Ray Green, the foreman of the woodshop. Ray Green took one look at me and a couple of other college kids and said, "Sure, I'll give you a job, but you'll be gone by the weekend." I spent a couple of days on an assembly line, two floors above the woodshop, before Ray Green figured out where he could use me. We were making Fun Time Ovens. Other assembly lines in the building were making foos ball and air hockey games. Mark Major, a high school basketball player who was a year younger than me and a sophomore that fall at St. Lawrence University, quit after the first few days. I would have been right behind him if Ray Green hadn't moved me off the assembly line. I had finally arrived, after seventeen years living there, at the heart of Amsterdam, working in one of the mills, if only for a college summer.

Since I had experience cutting wood with circular saws the summer before, Green took me off the assembly line and gave me my own machine. There was absolutely no skill involved. Everything was premeasured. All I had to do was slide a stack of particle board into a metal template on the table. The saw was mounted overhead. I held the wood with my left hand and pulled the saw with my right. The pieces were a foot and a half long and maybe four inches wide. I'd fit them onto the table three or four at a time, make a pass with the saw, then push the cut pieces to the side and throw the ends into a big plastic bin. Over and over again. When I had cut enough wood to fill the entire span of the metal table, I stacked the pieces on a pallet, loaded the left side of the table with uncut particle board, and went through the whole process again.

It was mesmerizing. Still, I liked the job better than the one on the assembly line, as I controlled my own machine and could take a break to use the bathroom or to get a drink of water whenever I wanted, as long as I made quota. There was also more variety in the work, what with the variation of having to stack the cut wood, load the uncut pieces onto the table, and then work the saw again. We also took breaks every now and then to shovel mounds of our own dust into the bins. We were told not to be too fussy shoveling sawdust. There were floor sweepers with higher standards who would come around behind us and ask us to step away from the saws. The trick was to make quota without cutting your fingers off. A couple of the foremen who'd come by to huddle with Ray Green sported the trademark of career carpenters, a few stubbed fingertips here and there, sometimes whole fingers clipped beneath the knuckle—nothing they seemed to worry about.

I worked in Building Six. I would walk a half an hour from my parents' house to get there before the 6:55 A.M. buzzer blew. The buzzer blew again at 7 A.M., when the saws would begin to hum. If I arrived a little early, I would lay down on the loading docks to take a five-minute nap. We had a ten-minute break at 10 A.M., half an hour at noon, and another ten minutes at 2 P.M. The shift let out at 3:30. We were paid for the ten-minute breaks, not for the half-hour lunch. We punched the clock four times a day: in the morning, at lunch, after the lunch break, and again at the end of the shift. I packed four sandwiches everyday, two for lunch and one for each ten-minute break.

I usually bought my drinks there, as it was a sweatshop. By lunchtime any drinks I brought from home were warm. There was a snack area, usually smoke-filled, with tables and vending machines, the one part of the factory other than the bathrooms where smoking was permitted. Anyone caught with a lit cigarette outside the snack room and bathroom was sure to lose his job, what with the sawdust and all. I usually ate my lunch as fast as I could, outside in the greater coolness of the loading dock, then hit the deck for a twenty-minute nap, a couple of blocks of wood for a pillow. If it were raining outside, I'd lay down on a six-foot pallet of particle board near the big table saw. There were no floor fans allowed in the building as they stirred up the dust. At least a couple guys on the floor missed work that summer with scratched corneas.

On the hottest days of July and August, Green and the other foremen would bring out large containers of salt tablets and place them by the water coolers. I followed the lead of some of the regulars who worked there year round and swallowed a couple whenever I saw them downing a few. We were required to wear protective headphones on our ears and many of us chose to wear goggles, though they were hot. Sweat stung my eyes and steamed the goggles up.

The only trouble I had with Ray Green that summer took place on the day he moved me to work at one end of a massive table saw. I insisted on wearing a face mask and he couldn't find one on the floor. I had heard that we were required by law to wear them. No one else on the floor had one on. As long as I worked on a band or circular saw I wasn't concerned, but the table saw was another story. I made an issue of it. I had to slide six-by-four pieces of particle board, stacked two boards high, onto a rack of rollers, then feed the boards into the mouth of the saw. Four saws ripped the board lengthwise into strips, and then a couple of saws came across the other way and cut the strips into pieces. It was easier to feed the boards into the saw than to work the other end, catching the cut pieces and stacking them as they came off the rollers. From my end, when the saw first bit into each board, it kicked back a cloud of dust. I was breathing the stuff. When I stopped work to ask for the mask, Green told me to go back to my saw. Then he brought a couple of other foremen along to work on me. They pointed out that no one else was wearing one, and there were some fifty people on the floor. I asked him if it were true that we were required by law to wear them.

"Okay, college boy," he said to me in disgust, "that's no law I know about. But I'll go get you one if it'll make you feel any better. I'll have to go clear over to another building. You know how much time you're wasting me? You think you're so much different than everyone else here? But that's okay. I'll get you one. You just keep on working till I do."

Some twenty minutes later, he tossed the mask and a couple of spare filters on a pallet near me and walked away.

I didn't miss any work that summer. I also put in four and a half hours overtime every Saturday and worked, on occasion, a couple extra hours at the end of a regular work day. The last day I was there, at the end of August, Ray Green came up to me during the 2 P.M. break and said, "You can have a job here anytime you want, college boy. Any summer you want, you just let me know." I waited until he was out of sight, then slipped off early, punched the clock, and felt as though I were escaping with my life.

That was one of the most boring stretches of my college years. I didn't see Marina for the entire months of June and July. I no longer enjoyed hanging out with the boys, drinking beer and smoking pot, in part because I didn't want to risk trouble with the police. I stayed at home with my parents and with my younger brother, who was seventeen and working in one of the other Coleco buildings, twelve-hour shifts, four days on, four days off. Mostly I read books and started doing one hundred pushups per day in two sets of fifty. Stacking all that wood was getting me into the best shape of my life. When my parents left to go to Martha's Vineyard for the month of August, I stayed home working for Ray Green. I wanted to make quota, not only at Coleco, but for my father and Amherst College. The Amherst financial aid director had already told me how much money he expected me to contribute from my summer's earnings. I intended to reach that goal. At $3.12 an hour, $124.80 per week, less taxes, plus four and a half hours each Saturday at $4.68 an hour, I had to work through August to give my father my share—a clean one thousand dollars.

20

The Fly

Marina and I continued to write to one another that summer and occasionally talked by phone. There was some Orthodox Jewish waiter at the resort hotel in the Catskills who felt that she was toying with me. By then, she was twenty-four years old. I was twenty. He thought she was afraid of a man her age or older. He was in graduate school at the Yeshiva University in New York. Though Marina's father was Jewish, her mother was a goyim like me. That made Marina a shiksa, unless she converted back to the faith. This rabbinical student had Marina listening carefully enough to relate everything he said in letters she wrote to me. In his view, anyway, I wasn't coming down to defend my territory. I clearly had other priorities. When my parents went away for the month of August, she agreed to come up to visit me one weekend and then didn't want to stay.

Marina arrived on a Saturday. I had put my overtime in at Coleco that morning. My brother was still out working his longer shift. We had the house to ourselves. She looked like someone out of the nineteenth century: long, black, ankle-length skirt, white blouse, nothing too revealing, her hair—brown, with a touch of red—held up in a bun by a wooden clasp, a hint of lipstick and no other makeup. A ring I had given her, too large for her finger, was flipped the wrong way around. There were flecks of paint, a veritable rainbow, on her rough hands. We drove out to the Auriesville Shrine, a lovely garden I thought Marina might like, and walked around and talked amidst the statues of the saints. She was beautiful, clothed or naked, and talented either way. She paid no money for the five years she spent at Cooper Union. She was a little out there, though, by my small-town standards.

Marina couldn't believe what I had done to myself, working in such an ugly place, in such an ugly town. She claimed people chose the lives they

157

led—that time and circumstance had very little to do with it. It was almost a religion with her. She offered me that wisdom with a fanaticism worthy of any Christian evangelical. Something in me had passively chosen this town, chosen this work in the factory. It was part of my being, or part of something my spirit required of me before I was even born, and it certainly *wasn't* her destiny. It was further evidence of something lazy in me that I had resigned myself to such a place. It was clear to her that I didn't have the courage to lead an artistic life. Her job as a waitress in the Catskills was no great shakes, but at least there were mountains and lakes nearby. At least there was beauty around her. At least some of the help were interesting people—artists up from New York City, or Orthodox Jews who believed consciously in a way of life, however strange it might seem to us, and consciously committed themselves to the act of living it.

It didn't much convince her that I was simply trying to raise a little money to help my father with tuition—that my job that summer was a stopgap measure, only a temporary situation that would lead to better things.

"You don't hear a word I'm saying," she said to me. "I am not talking about money."

I saw her again nine years later, at the Hungarian Café in New York City, across the street from St. John the Divine, corner of 112th and Amsterdam. She brought some slides of her paintings for me to see. I held them to the light, sure evidence of her talent. She seemed happy. She had found a partner by then, a sculptor who made his living as a stone mason. They lived in Vermont. They had no children. That earlier afternoon, at the Auriesville Shrine, whatever vision she had for herself contained no room for me. Maybe she knew me well enough to see that the job, the home, and the children I would have eventually required of myself I would have also required of her. I was a little relieved, a little sad too, when she dropped me off at my house and turned, full of a sense of her own destiny, toward the New York State Thruway, the Catskills, and then to some analogous place, distant from my life.

Murph and the boys couldn't understand, that summer, why I was no longer hanging out in the evening with them. It didn't bother them enough that they would actually call me on the phone to harangue me out. But

I would run into Murph or Woody from time to time, walking up and down Union Street, on the way to work and on the way home again. Rod was also working the first shift at Coleco that summer, in the print shop. Sometimes Rod and I would walk over to Murph's house after work and drag him down to The Annex for a beer. Afternoons were slow and dreamy in the aftermath of the workday, far more tame than The Annex's late-night scene. I remember one afternoon, drinking with Murph and Rod and Woody on a day that a boy, not yet sixteen, too young by law to be working at Coleco, stuck his head inside a molding machine when he couldn't get it to work and brushed against the switch. The molding rod caught him behind one ear, shot his head full of hot plastic. We heard the sirens at work. Word spread fast. There was a hush in the bar that afternoon as The Annex siphoned off the flow of pedestrians that made its way each day at 3:30 down the hill from Coleco. A thick silence set in, and then Rod, sitting at the bar with Woody and Murph and me, suddenly looked up and said, loud enough for everyone to hear,"The dumb fuck!" Then everyone started laughing, and someone racked up the pool table, and someone else started pumping quarters into the jukebox.

I also remember another afternoon when someone—I think it was Bobby Iacini—was sitting at the bar with Rod and me. Bobby and I had won one little league baseball championship together, during my second-to-last year on St. Agnello's. He was a year older than me and had lost part of one leg in a motorcycle accident, from the shin down. He peg-legged around with a gypsylike red bandana over his head. A couple years before, he received a $200,000 settlement from the accident and had already spent most of it.

If it was in fact Iacini sitting there in The Annex that day, he wanted to show Rod a trick. It was August. The door to the bar was open. Parked cars, most of them gas guzzlers built years before the oil embargo of the mid-1970s, lined both sides of the street. Along with the exhaust fumes that regularly drifted in, there was a fly buzzing around, occasionally landing on the bar. Bobby was the winning pitcher in our little league championship game. Whoever was sitting there, Bobby or someone else, had quick reflexes. He caught the fly midair and held it still buzzing in his fist.

Then he slam-dunked it into a glass of beer. Rod and I huddled over the glass to watch it swim around for awhile. Then Iacini said,

"Betcha I can make that fly fly again. Betcha I can bring it back."

The fly had stopped moving by now and Larry Lanzi came out from behind the bar to watch.

"All right," Rod said, "you're on. I'll bet you a beer."

"Lanz," Iacini said, "get me a spoon and that salt shaker over there."

Lanzi brought the spoon over. Iacini fished the fly out of the glass and dumped it onto the dry edge of a napkin. Then he covered the fly with a small mound of salt. The salt soaked the beer out of the insect's body. The fly began to shake a wing and then a couple of legs, and then actually began to crawl out of the salt mound.

Lanz said, "Look at that!"

I said, "I'll be damned!"

Iacini grinned. The fly was trying both wings out and looked like it was getting ready to lift off. Then Rod gave Iacini a look and said, "Iacini, you owe me a beer," and smeared the insect against the bar with the slap of a hand. "Bring back that!" Rod said, and we all laughed.

21

Good Friday

The next day was Good Friday. I woke early and ate in the hotel restaurant, an homage of sorts to Murph: two eggs and sausage, home fries, toast and coffee, just the sort of high-cholesterol special I used to track mornings, from diner to diner, in any city I ever called home. Murph started out his work life behind those double doors. It was a distant connection. I couldn't really feel him there as they swung and closed to orders of over easy and scrambled. To my surprise, at 7 A.M., there were a dozen other people scattered among the vinyl booths and wooden tables. The restaurant could probably seat fifty or more. Maybe Amsterdam was doing better than I thought. At least the Best Western was drawing traffic off the highway, though I bet I was the only guest who had been there for more than one night. I bet I was the only customer whose final destination was New York State Thruway Exit 27.

I huddled behind *The Collected Poems of Czeslaw Milosz* just to let the waitress know that I wasn't up for small talk. Milosz wasn't much of a conversation starter in Amsterdam, but during that week he was for me an inspiration, a Christian who was open to realities and to contradiction. I loved his poem "What I Learned from Jeanne Hersch," his defense of the violent nature of cats, and also his homage to Pope John Paul II. I loved his humility and sharp intellect—his ability to embrace the limitations of the human mind and to insist on its full capabilities too. I envied a man who could write, in his nineties, "Awakened," a prose poem in which "in advanced age, my health worsening," Milosz

> woke up in the middle of the night, and experienced a feeling of happiness so intense and perfect that in all my life I had only felt its premonition. And there was no reason for it. It didn't obliterate

161

consciousness; the past which I carried was there, together with its grief. And it was suddenly included, was a necessary part of the whole. As if a voice were repeating: "You can stop worrying now; everything happened just as it had to. You did what was assigned to you, and you are not required anymore to think of what happened long ago." The peace I felt was a closing of accounts and was connected with the thought of death. The happiness on this side was like an announcement of the other side. I realized that this was an undeserved gift and I could not grasp by what grace it was bestowed on me.

That sort of moment would be a real achievement in any life, quite apart from Milosz's literary feats. Milosz lived in Poland through World War II and then lived through the Russian Occupation. He experienced more violence than I could ever imagine. Maybe he felt good that he was on the right end of it, in the Polish Resistance. But he had his grief too and embraced it. I hoped, in that moment, during my breakfast on Good Friday, in Amsterdam, New York, in the building where Murph held his first job, that I might live with something close to that level of integrity. That in the end I might be able to say, *I was given only one life to live. I regret nothing. Here it is.*

The waitress left me alone, except to fill my cup. When I later married a Catholic, I was surprised to find that in Catholicism there is no Good Friday Mass. Not that I had any intention that evening of going to church. My coffee was about all I could take black that morning. Still, I remembered clearly the Good Friday service in my father's church, everyone, even the minister, dressed only in black, the acolytes, the choirmaster too, and the cross draped with it. Even the cough drops the men distributed were black licorice, the dirge of the choir in a minor key, with no organ accompaniment. It felt distinctly medieval. It felt like I was living for one evening per year in a monastery.

Mornings were always a meditative time for me, and all the more so on that Good Friday. My thoughts strayed only briefly to Golgotha. The seder the night before had given me my fill of the passion play. I had my own dark hour to deal with. I was four years divorced, a worried single father of two young children—an eleven-year-old girl and a seven-year-old boy,

both of them smart, physically beautiful, and gifted, musically and otherwise. I believed I had in me what they might need in a father, but I was a
lousy mother. For the past four years, in the summer, I fed them almost
completely off the grill. Now I had come home to look my past in the
eye. What could it offer me?

I headed back to my room with no intention of going anywhere until
that evening. My work habits were difficult, I was sure, for anyone to live
with: Given my druthers, I could spend whole days—whole weeks—
alone. I liked nothing better than to get up in the morning, without
speaking to anyone, and then to read and write for the entire day, without
once dealing with the dog or the dishes, or laundry, or any other human
trouble. But that sort of intense concentration wasn't much of a reality in
my life anymore, ever since my daughter was born. That morning at the
Best Western was my last day without my kids and I could already feel
the door closing on the final month of a spring 2003 sabbatical. I would
have growled at the waitress had she begun to chat with me.

Back in my room, I thought of David Dreaney's older brother, who
asked his childhood minister—my father—to visit him when he was dying
of AIDS in a hospital somewhere in western Massachusetts. This was a
story my father used to tell. Though he hadn't seen my father or even been
in a church in more than twenty years, a few days before he died the older
Dreaney boy told his former minister that only then did he realize the most
meaningful moments in his life occurred when he was a child, singing in
the St. Ann's choir. I didn't know the older Dreaney boy. I knew the
younger, a few years older than me. I remember him showing me his
ripped knuckles one night at church basketball practice. "That's where I
punched a guy in the mouth last night." I half believed him. They were
biological brothers, both adopted.

I worked, in my first job, with David Dreaney's fiancée, when I was
sixteen, at Grants Department Store, where I cut keys for customers as the
hardware part-time sales boy and sold wall paneling. Business was poor.
Time moved slowly in four-and-a-half-hour shifts. Whenever I had nothing to do the store manager told me to straighten and restraighten my
undisheveled shelves. The younger Dreaney's fiancée was a thin, tall girl,
with long blonde hair. She worked behind the jewelry counter. Even then

I thought she was much too quiet to handle David's fury. In a Volkswagen Bug, later that summer, on a back county road, David Dreaney tried to pass his fiancée and her mother on the right berm of the highway, just for a joke, and hit a coma he would never wake from in the form of a telephone pole.

"The end is in the beginning and lies far ahead," as Ralph Ellison puts it in *Invisible Man*. What a strange thing, when you think of it, to say about an adolescent boy, the subject, initially anyway, of Ellison's great novel. Where we are in the beginning is, in some real way, where we will end up. We think we leave things and people and places and experiences behind and then they boomerang around and catch us flush in the face. I think that Ellison means that, by the time you are eighteen, the foundation has already been laid. You are what your family and your home community and personal history, what your church and school and hometown have made you. Part of you will stay that way for your entire life no matter how much you change from place to place, or from job to job. What you are is what you will remain, at least in part, whether you choose eventually to return to your hometown, or, more likely, permanently to leave.

Ellison writes almost nothing about the church, except in the figure of Rinehart, his con man of a street preacher, but the phrase that interweaves the 550 pages of his book, like a jazz trumpeter picking up and handing off the melodic line, echoes Eliot's "Little Gidding." Ellison knew what he was doing, as there is a quote from Eliot at the beginning of his novel. But maybe Eliot's meaning dives deeper:

> the end of all our exploring
> Will be to arrive where we started
> And know the place for the first time.
> Through the unknown, remembered gate
> When the last of earth left to discover
> Is that which was the beginning.

I didn't know if David Dreaney's brother ever saw it in this way, but for my money, on that Good Friday, in Amsterdam, New York, part of the process of growing old was to find in the end always the beginning—a sense of home so strong that it is not only rooted in place and time, under the actual roof of a family house or temple, but also embedded so deeply in the self that you carry it with you everywhere you go.

And yet, for me, the unknown, remembered gate was the door to Brooks's cellar as well as the vestibule to my father's church. It was also New York State Thruway Exit 27.

22

Two Dogs

That night I drove over to Woody's home in Fort Hunter, six miles outside of Amsterdam. I had never been to that house before. Woody and his son Eric were shooting baskets outdoors when I drove up. Though Woody loved to talk about his own crazy years, he didn't want the same for his sons. He moved his kids to Fort Hunter where they went to the rural Perth rather than to the urban Amsterdam Public Schools. Woody bragged in front of his son that Eric had never beaten him one-on-one. That remark got nothing but a smile out of Eric. He looked more like a middle linebacker than a basketball player. Then Eric and a friend took off to hang out at a Stewart's Ice Cream Shop. Once Eric had gone, Woody told me that his sons never got into any kind of trouble:

"They go out for ice cream on a Friday night! They're wimps, but I'm not complaining!"

Then, as soon as we were inside, I realized I couldn't stay long. Woody invited me in to the snarl of his two dogs. He yelled at them both to "Shut the hell up!" but they kept barking and sizzling anyway.

"That one's all right. It's the other one I worry about." Both dogs were showing me their front teeth. "Don't worry, Harc, they won't go past the gate."

I sat down in the living room while Woody went to take a leak, the dogs behind the gate a few feet away. The living room was large enough for a couch, a couple of armchairs, and a computer desk. There was a small kitchen in the back, a bedroom off that, and a second floor. It was good to see that Woody was doing well.

The gate looked a little flimsy to me. It was one of those wooden, spring-mounted, toddler affairs. It wasn't even screwed in to the wall. The dogs kept spitting and growling. When Woody came back with two beers, I said,

"Wood, to be honest with you, I don't *do* attack dogs anymore."

"They're not attack dogs, Harc! That one's a baby. He just has to smell you. He's just growling 'cause the other one is. Here, let me show you."

"That's okay, Wood," I said, "They're just perfect right where they are." I wasn't, in that moment, only thinking of the well being of my children.

Woody opened the gate wider, kicked one dog back with his foot and grabbed the other by the collar. The dog he took out looked like a black Lab of some kind, seventy pounds or so. The other dog, about the same size, was a shepherd mix. The Lab kept barking and growling until he stuck his nose deep in my crotch. He took a good whiff and then shut up, though he kept trembling all over. The shepherd kept barking, even more wildly.

"I don't have to worry when the old lady's home alone with these two around. I trained 'em. *Shut the hell up!* Whenever anyone would knock at the door, I'd say, *'What's that?! Who's that?!'* Over and over again till they got the picture. They're smart. They caught on quick."

"Yeah, well, how do they know when the person knocking at the door is your friend?"

"They let me figure that. They just don't want anything to happen to me."

"Nothing is going to happen to you, Wood."

"Yeah, but they don't know that. You afraid of these dogs, Harc?" He pushed the Lab with the flat of his foot, lightly in the butt. "They won't bother you while I'm here, although that one bit Van Epps in the ass one time." Woody laughed. It worried me that Woody found that funny.

"Outside, Wood. I'm drinking the beer *outside."*

On the way out through the kitchen, Woody stopped to show me the cabinets he put in *for the old lady.* Outside, his seven-year-old daughter moved to the neighbor's driveway to make room for us. Woody and I shot at the hoop above his garage door. Woody could still nail a twenty-foot jump shot, but he told me he didn't really play anymore, except to fool around with the boys. His daughter kept yelling from the neighbors' driveway:

"Daddy, watch me! Daddy, watch!" She was throwing the ball two-hand underhand at the basket and missing the rim by a good two feet.

"Okay, hon, okay! That's real good, sweetie!" Woody said, without ever really looking over. Woody told me by phone, some years ago, after Gina had left and he was living alone with the boys, that he would never get married again. He claimed he would *live* with his girlfriend but not marry her, if it ever came to that. By then, Woody had already met his second wife. She was working at a Cumberland Farms convenience store as a cashier. Though I don't remember her, she was the homecoming queen in the class ahead of us, during her senior year. Woody married her when she became pregnant with their daughter. During my week in Amsterdam, on both nights Woody and I drank beer, she was working as a waitress at the Armory Grill.

Then Woody told me about the one time Eric had an accident—how it cost him six hundred dollars to pay the traffic fine, the tow, and his share of the insurance costs. He told me how he used to bust Eric's ass all the time—*ya cost me six hundred dollars!*—laughing all the while. That was the worst trouble Eric had ever been in.

Woody would never be Phil Fucking Donahue. If he was ever given the chance, he'd never wow Oprah or Oprah's Dr. Phil. Among the more dedicated fathers I've known, I rank my brother Tom, who has an autistic child at home. I also count Woody among that number, on the basis of sheer tenacity. He would never leave his kids. You would have to kill him first.

When Gina left him, she gave him care of their two boys for awhile, then later sued him for custody. Woody paid ten thousand dollars in legal fees and won in court. Though no one asked him, he insisted on accepting only half the child support offered by the judge. That act of chivalry didn't put him in any kind of good standing with Gina, or stop him from calling her repeatedly a pain-in-the-ass type A.

"Don't let the dogs out, hon. Be sure to shut the door!" Woody yelled as his daughter left the neighbors' court to head back inside. "Okay, Daddy!" she yelled back, the door bouncing off the side of the house. It rebounded against the doorframe and hung half open. Distantly, I could hear the dogs going at it again.

"Hon, I said to be sure to shut the door!" She was already out of earshot as Woody clicked the side door back into its frame.

"Woody, I think I had better take off," I said. I had barely finished my beer.

"Don't worry, Harc! They won't come out."

"That's okay, Wood. I'm not worried about the dogs. I have to pick up my kids tomorrow." I could feel Ohio pulling on me. I told him it was great seeing him again, but I had a good five-hundred-mile drive the next day. Woody walked me to the car.

"Okay, Harc! Okay, Buddy! Just let me know if you're ever back in town."

It seemed like the same story, twenty-eight years of circling back to Amsterdam to see my oldest friends, until I could stand no more and had to leave again. Once gone, I had to come back, just to remind myself of realities. Sure, I had become accustomed to—in Frank's view of things— "rich, upper-class sons of a bitches," in part because I had come from that milieu and—sure as I was cut from my father's clerical cloth—had finally become one myself. In Frank's classification of the human species, that designation included just about anyone who held a white-collar job and owned his own home. Frank had enough of an influence on me that I was not entirely comfortable attending a private college, or even a state university, much less teaching in one. Even now, during my own committee and department meetings, I can hear Frank's anarchic urge whispering in my ear, laughing at the public posture of every single faculty member, myself included, every administrator.

As I drove the next morning to Rochester, New York, to pick up my children, I realized fully well that my trip to Amsterdam was part of this larger pattern of circling back. When I left Amsterdam for what I thought was the last time, after my summer in the Coleco wood shop, I didn't live at home with my parents again, but I kept finding my way back to town. When my parents first moved into the Adirondacks, I'd come home to visit them and then head down to see Woody and the boys.

Later, when I was a lecturer at Tufts, I spent the large part of one summer near them, in an Adirondack cabin with no running water.

Whatever writing I managed to do during those cool summer months I long ago threw away. It was 1987. I was thirty years old. Woody was still married to Gina, still living in a trailer outside of Amsterdam. Their son Eric must have been two. His brother Scottie was a baby. We spent one night in Rod's backyard, smoking joints. When I stopped by early to pick Woody up in my 1974 Chevy Nova, he got in the car and said, "I'm going to get *twisted* tonight," and laughed. Then every time I cracked open a beer, all night long, he asked me over and over again,

"Who's driving, Harc? Who's driving?" as if he didn't feel entirely at ease with where the drift of the evening was taking him.

"What are you, paranoid, Wood?" I shot back at him.

"I just want to know who's driving. What d'ya think, I don't want to live see my kids grow?"

I was supposed to spend that night at Woody's so I wouldn't have to drive forty-five miles up a sleepy state highway to Wells, New York. When we pulled in at 3 A.M., Gina was throwing fistfuls of Woody's clothes out into their front yard. I sobered up, drove north, and left Woody alone to face Gina's anger. Woody had been out of work for a long time. I later heard from him that Gina held me at least partially responsible for bringing her husband home that night, stoned and drunk at such a late hour.

Then there was my first wedding, in my father's church. Murph came down from Vermont, Frank drove up from South Carolina, Woody, Gina, and Rod were still in town. My old roommate from Amherst, Joe Manges, flew up from New Mexico with his wife. Another roommate—Bill Cohn, my best man in my second wedding—and his wife Sue Dahl, who I also knew from Amherst, drove in from Boston. I seated the Amherst group with writer and graduate school friends—Brady Earnhart, a classmate from the Iowa Workshop who later became a terrific songwriter, his lover Doug, and two poet friends from Boston—Gian Lombardo and my old teacher Harold Bond. My first marriage was to a woman from halfway around the world, a gifted composer and native of Beijing—no more un- stable than many of the more talented American artists I met when I was a fellow at Yaddo and at the MacDowell Arts Colony. Though we seated the college boys separately from the Amsterdam crowd, all the disparate pieces of myself gathered around those tables.

That was the last time I saw Murph and Frank—they nailed my car with shaving cream and papier-mâché. It was also the last time I saw my Uncle Otis, a man who knew something about laughter. His real name was Erastus Otis Haven, *the third.* He was my father's first cousin. He lived on Martha's Vineyard in a house he built himself, retired early, practiced TM, and much to my father's dismay turned away from his Episcopal roots in favor of the Unitarian Church. My aunt called him Bud. He had been in remission from bone cancer for a decade and died within the year.

My old choirmaster, my father's church organist, played the wedding. My mother and he had never resolved their constant dissonance during my father's twenty-eight-year tenure at the church. For years, the choirmaster drank too much and never quit chain smoking. Mrs. Davies, my father's secretary, was also there, a lovely woman who knew the local scene. She sat near my parents' table. She had tried throughout my teenage years to warn my father that I was hanging out with a tough crowd. If only for a moment, Mrs. Davies and the rest of the St. Ann's parishioners lifted their glasses and drank at long last in unison with the Koller 49ers.

Earlier, during the ceremony, my ex-wife wouldn't stop talking on the altar. I had to keep shushing her. My nephews, the ring bearers, mistakenly switched the cushions. My father tried to place a ring meant for my finger on my ex-wife's extended hand. That was a bad sign, my ex-wife told me in broken English, right there on the altar. She all but said the marriage was cursed as we knelt at the communion rail and waited for the bread and wine. Even these years later, I try to hush her in that moment. Though I can't speak for her, my hope is that she sees, despite any turbulence, only lovely energies emerging from those mistaken rings. Our daughter was born two years later in the Beijing Capital Hospital, our son Jonah, an Ohio boy, waiting in the wings for four years more. It was September 9, 1989, and unseasonably hot. After the reception, half the wedding party, the bride and groom among them, peeled off their clothes and jumped into the Sacandaga.

23

Exit 27

My last day in Amsterdam, Saturday, April 19, 2003, as I turned west on the New York State Thruway, I planned to propose to another woman—Terri—though I hadn't yet told my children. I thought I would wait until July to ask her, and then, if she agreed, wait another year for the ceremony. The curves of the Mohawk paralleled the highway. The river wove in and out of view, well past Utica, for sixty miles or so. I picked my children up from my ex-wife's apartment in Rochester and had them home for Easter, in a church where they both sang and played in bell choirs. One week later, Terri and my kids and some of her children gathered in St. Luke's Episcopal Church, in Granville, Ohio, where my father had just begun to work as interim rector. He was seventy-seven years old. My mother greeted us at the door in her choir robe.

I left the church when I first left Amsterdam, except to attend services my father led when I was visiting home. Though I would occasionally wander over to St. John the Divine for vespers when I was a graduate student in New York, for all intents and purposes I was absent for seventeen years. My daughter Sarah brought me back again. I think that change in me must have surprised my first wife. From the time Sarah was one year old I took her with me, alone every Sunday, to the Episcopal service at St. Matthew's Church, in Ashland, Ohio. I thought she needed to go. I didn't know where else in America she might find some way to mature into her full nature, with a little spirit to leaven our national corporate bread.

She was a natural—sitting calmly through an hour-long service before she was two years old. There was no child care in that small Episcopal parish, so Sarah stayed with me in the pew. My plan was to drill old hymns so deeply inside of her that if she ever needed to access them again, *the still point of the turning world* would be waiting somewhere within her. Each week I tried to give her, even as a toddler, a quiet ceremonial moment, if only for an hour. I soon realized I was not going to church each Sunday for my daughter only.

Then there was the skepticism and wonder of my son Jonah, not yet three, sitting with me, with Sarah, with one of my Chinese students, and with my father and sister in a church in Beijing. One year before I thought I would ever need to remarry. My father and sister were visiting China for three weeks. I was at the end of a Fulbright year teaching American literature at Beijing Normal University. My student invited us to visit her Chinese parish. Jonah had not been in a church for the entire year we were in Beijing. He had no memory of ever having been in one. He looked around the packed pews, looked around again, the church so crowded that they had to bring folding chairs out to the sidewalks. TV monitors overhead, the surge of the city a few feet away—diesels, cars, handcarts, bicycles. A hymn began, in its native tongue, half the world away. Then to the utter hilarity of especially my student, Jonah, precocious boy, looked around again and said, "Where's God? Where's God, Dad?"—as if he expected to find him somewhere nearby, eating a bowl of noodles or drinking a cup of tea. Then he pointed and wondered if it might be the robed woman at the end of the procession. Maybe we gave him the answer he was after in the delight of our shared laughter.

Then two months before Terri and I were married, the *Amsterdam Evening Recorder* ran an article on my book of poems, *The Long Silence of the Mohawk Carpet Smokestacks*. Donny Overbaugh read the piece and gave me a call. We talked for over an hour. He told me he didn't recognize me at all from the photograph. We joked about playing tackle football in the street, in winter, both of us with knee problems now. OB told me he would do it all over again. He had taken over his parents' gift shop once his stepfather died. He ran it for his mother but didn't know the suppliers in the way that his stepfather had. The shop went down the tubes.

Donny also told me what I already knew: Danny Agresta was dead. He came down with cancer, of one sort or another, and stopped by ghostlike to see Overbaugh a month before he died. Now OB was having his own troubles. He had applied for Social Security disability insurance.

The application process was slow. Since he had never worked a regular job, he never paid into the system. He was just trying to get through the summer. He was pretty sure that by fall he would start receiving government checks. His girlfriend was supporting him, though she had her own kids to worry about. Donny had a few children, too, by an earlier marriage. I didn't know, exactly, whether he was asking me for help. I kept thinking of my own two children and of Terri's four—*six college educations.* I called him Donny. He called me Harc. He told me that no one had called him anything other than OB or Donald in twenty-five years.

For days after I hung up the phone, I was back again. We were all playing some board game in my second-floor bedroom, the side porch off my room open to June. Where was the justice in it all? I owned a spacious, colonial home in a small quiet town, where I worked only eight months of the year. I had a beautiful woman in my life, a whole boatload of children. My yard was an acre large. For days after Donny's call, I could hear, beneath the banter of all those children, the thrum of the unemployed, the long imprisoned, and the long dead boy.

But mainly I remember the freedom of my first escape and the melodrama of my return. I hitchhiked out of town the day after my last high school class and bounced home again late that summer, if only to pack for college. Though I would come down with mono in August and was still a little shaky on the day of my arrival at Amherst College, I was headed to some sort of paradise—I was sure—where people sat around under the trees talking of poetry and philosophy. That illusion came to a quick halt the moment I attended my first mixer, my first frat party. Still, there would be no early pregnancy to derail me, no shotgun marriage, no charge for drunk driving or for possession or sale of marijuana. That it might have been otherwise, I knew too well. That day I left for college, Fate and Freedom were fighting it out again, and Freedom had just taken the upper hand.

Then I hitchhiked home for my first Thanksgiving vacation. During the next four years my father left me largely to my own devices to make my way back for Christmas and other holidays. It was a two-and-a-half-hour drive from campus. I didn't have much money. With some luck I was able to thumb it in less than four hours. As a young man my father once hitchhiked from Albany to Seattle, then took a boat north to work a summer on the Alaskan Railroad. He thought nothing of my desire to make my own way home. I thought I had ventured out. I had been places: 120 miles east to Massachusetts.

After catching my last ride, all those college years, I'd walk down the I-90 exit ramp, past the ticket booth where my friend Steven DiBacco, a New York State Thruway employee, would eventually stick his hand one too many times into the till. Once Steven was gone, as Exit 27 opened toward Market Street and to the city tucked on the north side of the Mohawk, I waved hello to DiBacco's abandoned toll. I half expected Frank and Donny O, Mr. K, Mrs. Johnson, Woody, Rat and Joe Battag, Mr. Sculco, Murph, Mary, Dowski and Bean—one or all of them, *someone* to come out from behind the Sleepy Dutchman Motel to greet this traveler home. Though no one was ever there, I heard them anyway, a few hundred yards south of the river, calling to me, singing my name.